הגדת אתיופיה

THE KOREN ETHIOPIAN HAGGADA:
JOURNEY TO FREEDOM

הוצאת קורן ירושלים

הגדת אתיופיה

The Koren Ethiopian Haggada:
Journey to Freedom

The Gould Family Edition

הגדה של פסח

בשילוב

מורשת יהודי אתיופיה
וסיפור יציאת אתיופיה

בעריכת
הרב מנחם ולדמן

Celebrating Ethiopian Jewish History,
Traditions & Customs

Edited by
Rabbi Menachem Waldman

Translated by
Binyamin Shalom

Koren Publishers Jerusalem

The Koren Ethiopian Haggada: Journey to Freedom
The Gould Family Edition
Celebrating Ethiopian Jewish History, Traditions & Customs

Edited by Menachem Waldman

Koren Publishers Jerusalem Ltd.
POB 4044, Jerusalem 91040, Israel
Tel: 972.2.633.0533 Fax: 972.2.633.0534
POB 8531, New Milford, CT 06776-8531, USA

www.korenpub.com

ISBN 978-965-301-292-9 *hardcover*
Printed in Israel

In loving memory of
our wonderful Grandmothers

Yvonne Clarke and Joyce Gould

Always in our thoughts
at this special time

הגדה של פסח

TABLE OF CONTENTS

The creation of a Passover Haggada that would include the traditions and heritage of Ethiopian Jewry alongside the story of the exodus from Ethiopia represents the fulfillment of a dream that was years in the making.

The chronicles of Ethiopian Jewry and their particular Jewish heritage flowed for many generations through channels that were set quite apart from all other Jewish communities. Linking them up once more with the main arteries of the life of the Jewish nation is one of the many miracles of the ingathering of exiles.

We have entered the times that the prophet Jeremiah prophesied, days that would overshadow even the tale of the Exodus from Egypt: "Therefore, behold, days are coming, says the Lord, when they shall no more say, 'As the Lord lives, who brought up the children of Israel out of the land of Egypt; but, As the Lord lives, who brought up and who led the seed of the House of Israel out of the north country, and from all countries into which I have driven them; and they shall dwell in their own land.'" (Jeremiah 23:7–8)

The Jews of Ethiopia earned their share of the land of Israel through innocent sacrifice and a full measure of trials and tribulations. On their journey through Sudan, thousands of community members died in so many forgotten places, without any sign or testament, their passing marked only by the searing pain burnt into the hearts and minds of the survivors. The Jews who made *aliya* from Ethiopia experienced their own version of the "desert generation" of the Bible – in Sudan.

As they joined the rest of the communities who made *aliya* to the Holy Land, a new chapter was inaugurated in the annals of the nation of Israel. The tale that comprises this particular chapter has taken pride of place in our time, while the tale of the Exodus from Egypt so many years before has taken a backseat (see *Berakhot* 12b).

In the Ethiopian Haggada you have before you, I have attempted to incorporate original source material from the heritage and traditions of Ethiopian Jewry alongside the traditional text of the Passover Haggada. I have chosen texts that relate to the Passover Holiday, the Haggada Seder, the story of the Exodus from Egypt, Hallel prayers, and thanksgiving to the Lord of Israel. In parallel to the aforementioned materials, I have chosen to include documents that reflect the redemption of Ethiopian Jewry, which stretches from their survival in exile and their longing to return to Zion through the relationships formed between the Ethiopian community and world Jewry from the nineteenth century up to the story of the journey and *aliya* to the land of Israel in the latter half of the twentieth century.

Alongside the written sources and the oral traditions that were subsequently recorded, photographs, which constitute significant evidence of the community's heritage, have been included together with the story of their redemption.

I have made an attempt to weave together all the sources such that the twin exoduses from Egypt and Ethiopia might intertwine.

In creating the present Ethiopian Haggada, I had in mind three objectives.

The first of these was to help introduce Ethiopian Jewry and its particular traditions into the mainstream of Jewish communal heritage. There is nothing like the Haggada and the Seder night to unite all the Jews of the world around a singular experience of their Jewishness. From this point on, the heritage of Ethiopian Jewry will have its place at the Seder table and on the shelves of Jewish homes.

The second objective is contained in the words of the Torah: "And thou shalt relate to thy son on that day, saying, 'This is done because of that which the Lord did to me when I came out of Egypt.'" (Exodus 13:8). It is as though we have been commanded to relate to our children our particular generation's tale of the Exodus from Egypt and to give thanks to God Almighty for keeping His promise to the people of Israel when He fulfilled that promise before our very eyes in gathering up His children from the Ethiopian lands.

The third objective of the present Haggada is directed at our brethren, the Ethiopian Jews themselves. Their heritage and past is a mystery to many of their community's own members. Reestablishing a connection with their roots and their Jewish spirit – which was steadfastly preserved with great sacrifice throughout many generations – will provide them with much-needed inspiration as they adapt to life in the Land of Israel.

Only time will tell if the Ethiopian Haggada will become a regular feature at the Seder table among our families, and whether the prayers, heritage and traditions that were previously observed and practiced in the community's villages will be revived and renewed once more among world Jewry.

I would like to thank the people at Koren Publishers Jerusalem greatly for rising so willingly to the challenge and taking the project upon themselves as a particularly Jewish mission. They also deserve our appreciation for their dedication in fashioning an original, precise, high-quality Passover Haggada that is both physically beautiful and spiritually enlightening at the same time.

For thirty years now I have been working at establishing connections: connecting Ethiopian Jewry to the very heart and soul of the Jewish people, creating a bridge between Ethiopian heritage and the traditions of the other religious streams of Judaism, bringing Ethiopian Jews back into the fold and assisting in the *aliya* and emigration of the remainder of the Ethiopian Jews.

In the hope that the Ethiopian Haggada will be welcomed as a fitting family Haggada and a source of spiritual inspiration, I pray for the strengthening and reinforcement of the bonds that unite us all as one nation under God.

Menachem Waldman

Kes Abba Yitzchak with the author, Atlit, 1983

The religious traditions of the members of the community of *Beta Israel* set them apart as a special group within Ethiopia, a community which acted on the one hand, in accordance with the Torah of Moses, and on the other hand, as a completely separate stream within the greater Jewish nation, observing a Jewish tradition all their own.

The complete detachment from the rest of the Jewish nation – which persisted for many generations – along with the complete absence of rabbinic literature and law, and the ongoing difficulties associated with survival in the midst of the dominant Christian Ethiopian majority all led to the formation of a unique Jewish heritage that does not have a parallel in any other community of the Jewish Diaspora. In the Ethiopian Jewish heritage, religious life is grounded in the written Torah, accompanied by oral commentaries that were passed

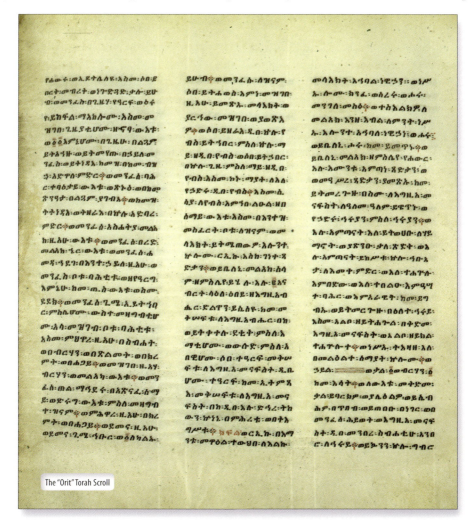

The "Orit" Torah Scroll

down from generation to generation, along with a handful of texts which were sacred to the community.

The commandments of the Torah were observed, however their observance was carried out in ways that differed greatly in their details from the customs common among all other Jewish communities and lacked all connection to the rabbinic legal tradition. The primary principles of faith were identical to those of historical Judaism: the belief in the God of Israel, the oneness of God, Israel as a chosen people based on the Torah and commandments that were given at Mount Sinai, acceptance of the

A *Nidda* Hut

prophets, reward and punishment, the world to come, heaven and hell, the ingathering of the exiles, and the coming of the messiah.

The members of the community observed a religious lifestyle, however only the priests of the community, *kessim*, and their intimate assistants among the elders of the community knew the explanations behind the commandments, replete with all their textual sources and traditional justifications. Religious life was based to a great extent on the guidance of the priest and his instruction. The members of the community would participate in prayer services by merely answering "Amen" and would perform such fundamental commandments as avoiding any labor on the Sabbath, observing laws of ritual purity and impurity, and only consuming meat that had been slaughtered by the priests. The Holy Scripture, including the Pentateuch, Prophets and Writings along with all the prayers, were in the Ge'ez tongue, an ancient Ethiopian language generally understood only by the priests and a few select elders. Many other commandments, such as donning

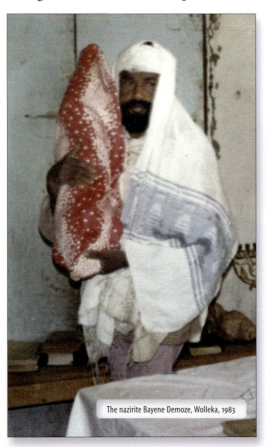

The nazirite Bayene Demoze, Wolleka, 1983

phylacteries, affixing a *mezuza* to the doorpost, or blowing the *shofar*, were not observed.

The Jews in Ethiopia maintained a strict distance from the non-Jews in the country and were diligent in avoiding all contact with any impure objects, in addition to taking ritual baths in natural springs for the purpose of ritual purification. In every village there was a *Nidda* hut, where the women would live throughout the period of their ritual impurity. In the past, congregations were accustomed to offering sacrifices on an altar that adjoined the community synagogue. Until very recently, several communities still maintained red heifer ashes, which the priests would prepare for the purpose of ritual purification after being exposed to contact with the dead.

The religious lifestyle of Ethiopian Jewry was thus characterized by the observance of

The Sigd Holiday, Ambover, 1957

traditions that had passed orally or visually from generation to generation, and were not based on the traditional learning associated with the interpretation of the written Torah, the rabbinic literature, and the legal texts

Emissaries from Israel demonstrating ritual slaughter, Ambover, 1976

Ritual slaughter for a *Tazkar* (memorial service), Biliboah, 1937

from other Jews around the world began to infiltrate the community. Thus they began to pray in the manner accepted throughout the larger Jewish community and adopted such traditions as the prayer shawl and phylacteries. However, these influences were minimal in scope and only reached a few select communities in the Gondar region. The greater Ethiopian Jewish community continued to practice their religion as it had been handed down from generation to generation.

The tens of thousands of survivors from the Ethiopian Jewish community (the "Falashmura") who emigrated to Israel from the year 1993 onward returned from their Christian ways to Judaism and a Jewish way of life while they were waiting to go on *aliya* in the centers set up for that express purpose in Addis Ababa and Gondar. At these centers, Jewish congregational life was observed in accordance with common Jewish law, under the guidance of rabbis and instructors from Israel.

Upon making *aliya* to Israel, the new arrivals encountered the religious traditions

published over the years. They were possessed by an innocent faith in the God of Israel, and determined to safeguard the Jewish religion in the traditions that had been passed down by their forefathers. Their survival in the very heart of Ethiopia is a veritable miracle. Down to the most recent generations, their religious leaders succeeded in passing on their Jewish heritage despite the difficult living conditions in Ethiopia.

From the second half of the nineteenth century onward, several events and developments took place in the areas where the Jews dwelled, which caused severe damage to their religious lifestyle. Many of the members of the community converted to Christianity, the standing of the religious leaders, nazirites, and priests was diminished, and as members began to turn to secular education and migrate to the larger cities, their religious observance waned as their assimilation within the larger Ethiopian community increased.

In the twentieth century, Jewish influences

Prayer on the Day of Remembrance for Those Lost in Sudan, Jerusalem, 2007

common in the land, and were presented with an entirely new reality wherein a large number of Jews were completely non-observant. At the same time, the priests of the community saw their influence severely diminished. The Ethiopian immigrants are currently undergoing the process of assimilating into Israeli society and putting down roots in the Holy Land. Their religious heritage, which had been safeguarded for many generations in Ethiopia, began to experience a profound spiritual crisis as it seemed incapable of continuing, and the elders of the community were no longer able to find a common language in which to communicate with the younger generation.

However, at the same time, a reciprocal relationship began to spring up in Israel between the traditions of Ethiopian Jewry and the traditions customary in Israel: learning from the elders began to incorporate the traditional learning of Mishna and Gemara, the consumption of meat slaughtered by the priests began to incorporate reliance on rabbinic certification of properly slaughtered meat, the Sabbath as it was observed in Ethiopia began to incorporate the rules of Sabbath observance common in the greater Jewish community, priestly prayer services evolved into prayers offered in the local neighborhood synagogue, and the observance of ritual purity and impurity began to incorporate the traditional laws of family purity observed in the land of Israel.

The transfer from Ethiopia to Israel took a heavy toll on the ancient traditions and heritage of the community. However, our Ethiopian brethren are no longer living in exile in the Ethiopian Diaspora. They are now located deep within the very heart and soul of the Jewish nation and the land of Israel, and they are moving forward along with the rest of the community in maintaining the Jewish essence of the Jewish people.

Matzot being baked by the congregation waiting to make *aliya* from Gondar, 200

THE PASSOVER HOLIDAY, PASIKA,
IN ACCORDANCE WITH ETHIOPIAN JEWISH TRADITIONS

The New Month of Nisan

At the start of every new month, the community would celebrate the Festival of the Moon and all labor would be forbidden on that day.

The celebration for the new month of Nisan, also known in the community as *Lisan*, traditionally marked the start of the calendar for all months, as it is written in the Torah: "This month shall be to you the beginning of months: it shall be the first month of the year to you" (Exodus 12:2). There were many prayers particular to this day and it was marked by the joyful consumption of meat. In the past, it was also common to offer a sacrifice. There was a widespread belief that anyone who properly celebrated the new month of Nisan would merit a good year, and whoever failed to celebrate the new month would have a terrible year.

The priests of the community blessed the congregation that they might have a good month, full of joy, and they would speak to the assembled members about the Passover holiday and the necessary preparations involved in its approach.

Choosing the Lamb for the Passover Sacrifice

In accordance with Ethiopian Jewish tradition, sacrifices were offered, however, in recent generations the only sacrificial custom still observed was the offering of the Passover sacrifice, which was commonly practised throughout the community.

About a week or two prior to the holiday, the members of the congregation would choose a young, male lamb to serve as the

Preparing the matza, Wolleka, 1984

Passover sacrifice, overseen by the priest. If they could not find a suitable lamb then they would choose a goat. They tried to see to it that the sacrificial lamb would be either completely white or brown, neither spotted nor black. The lamb was checked thoroughly to ensure that it bore no blemish. It was purchased on behalf of the entire congregation and kept until the appointed time of the sacrifice on the eve of the Passover holiday.

The Prohibition of Ḥametz

Any food product that had soured, fermented, or aged was considered Ḥametz as prohibited by the Torah. Accordingly, all sorts of grains that had been processed, milk which had been left standing or turned into cheeses, sparkling or alcoholic beverages, and essentially anything that had been left overnight, was forbidden to be eaten.

In the days leading up to the holiday, the houses and their environs would be cleansed of all Ḥametz and dirt. The utensils used for cooking and eating throughout the year were cleansed thoroughly and put away and new utensils were made for Passover. As the holiday drew near, all clothing was washed and the people cleansed themselves and took ritual baths.

The Baking of Matzot

Matza (known as *kita*) was made from wheat flour preferably, however it could also be prepared using kernels of *tef* (a type of grain used to prepare the traditional Ethiopian bread, *injera*), rice, or chickpeas.

The kernels were carefully sifted and great care was taken to ensure that they did not come into any contact with water. They were then ground using millstones that had been checked very well and thoroughly cleansed. The flour

Passover matza, Wolleka, 1984

was then placed in a new linen sack and set aside in a safe place until the holiday.

The matzot were prepared diligently and quickly: the flour was quickly mixed with water and a touch of salt, then the dough was poured onto a flat, clay pan, *megogo*, that rested over fiery coals.

The matzot were consumed soon after they were baked and were not left over till the next day.

The Passover Fast

On the fourteenth day of the month of Nisan, the day before the holiday, the Passover Fast would take place. The Fast was intended to be observed by firstborn sons and was known as the Fast of the Firstborn. Sometimes adults who were not firstborn children would also fast, particularly if they were fathers of firstborn sons.

Offering the Passover Sacrifice

After midday on the day before the Passover holiday towards sunset, the priest would slaughter the Passover sacrifice. Right by the

synagogue, there was a special place set aside and dedicated for use as the altar. The spot was marked with stones and was regarded as a holy place throughout the year.

The knife used for slaughtering the sacrifice was considered one of the holy items of the priest and was kept in a special place, generally located within the synagogue.

The lamb would be led to the altar, bound, and have its head placed to face the rising sun, which was also considered to be the direction in which Jerusalem lay.

The elders of the community would place their hands on the sacrifice and offer a mound of salt. The priest would sprinkle the salt over the body of the sacrifice from head to tail, re-

cite the blessing and pray that the sacrifice be accepted by the Lord and then slaughter it.

Fresh cut, leafy branches would be placed by the neck of the sacrifice so that the blood would not splash. The blood would be directed into a ditch that had been dug into the ground, and then covered over. The blood that remained on the leaves would be sprinkled in the doorway to the synagogue.

Following the ritual slaughter, the skin would be removed from the animal and the fat and the sciatic nerve would be removed (the nerve which runs through the rear thigh of an animal, whose consumption is forbidden according to the Torah). The meat of the sacrifice would be cut into large pieces, divided at the

Ritual slaughter at the hands of the community priest, Ambover, 1976

joints (taking care not to break any bones in the middle), and then roasted whole (including the head and the innards) over a central fire for the entire congregation.

If Passover eve fell on a Friday or Sabbath, they would not bring the sacrifice so as not to desecrate the Sabbath.

Consumption of the Passover Sacrifice

On the night of Passover, following the roasting of the sacrificial meat, salt would be sprinkled over it, and it would be divided among the members of the community who were pure at the time – both men and women – each member receiving a little bit of meat.

There were those who would consume the meat in the same manner that our ancestors consumed the Passover sacrifice in Egypt, as it is described in the Torah: "And thus shall you eat it: with your loins girded, your shoes on your feet, and your staff in your hand; and you shall eat it in haste; it is the Lord's Passover"

(Exodus 12:11). This was the very manner in which they would consume the sacrificial meat; the men would hold their canes in their hands, crouching down on bended knees, and the women would eat with young children strapped to their backs, as though they were about to set out on their journey.

At the time of the consumption of the sacrificial meat, the matza and *maror* (*merara* – bitter herbs) would also be eaten. They traditionally used the *gesho* plant or some other bitter herb.

Upon completing the meal they would wash their mouths and hands. Late in the night, all that was left of the sacrifice would be burned in the fire, including the skin and bones, so that nothing would be left over till the morning.

The Story of the Exodus from Egypt

On the night of Passover the priests and elders would tell the congregation the story of the Exodus from Egypt, though there was no set text to be recited like the standard Passover Haggada.

After recounting various stories related to the Exodus from Egypt, the women and children would return to their homes, and the adult men would accompany the priest to pray in the synagogue. Throughout the night they would thank the Lord for redeeming His people from Egypt and splitting the Red Sea, and they would offer special prayers related to the Passover holiday.

The Holiday and Hol HaMo'ed

The first day and the seventh day of the Passover holiday were holy days when all forms of labor were prohibited, with the exception of any work associated with the preparation of food.

There were those who strictly consumed only matza throughout the festival and avoided even meat to emphasize the commandment to consume matza all seven days. On the other hand, there were those who specifically encouraged the consumption of all sorts of permissible foods, including meat, in order to celebrate the Passover holiday.

During the days of Ḥol HaMo'ed, no work was performed, although trips were often taken to visit relatives.

The prayers during the holiday referred to the redemption from Egypt and the splitting of the Red Sea, and were accompanied by drums and other musical instruments.

The Conclusion of the Seventh Day of the Passover Holiday

At the conclusion of the seventh day of the Passover holiday, Ḥametz would still not be consumed, however they would begin to pre-pare the *injera*, the traditional Ethiopian bread made from *tef* fermented in water.

The next day they would quickly prepare the bread, making either *injera* or *dabo*, made from wheat or barley dough, though other grains might also be used.

The first piece of bread to be baked, along with a sparkling beverage that was hastily prepared, would be given as a gift to the priest or elder, who would bless the bread, break it and then let it be known that from this point forward the consumption of Ḥametz was permissible. As the priests recited the blessing, the entire congregation would recite the Ten Commandments from memory.

The Counting of the Omer

With regard to the counting of the days of the Omer, it is written in the Torah: "And you shall count for yourselves from the morrow after the Sabbath, from the day that you brought the omer of the wave offering; seven complete Sabbaths shall there be: to the morrow after the seventh Sabbath shall you number fifty days and you shall offer a new meal offering to the Lord" (Leviticus 23:15–16). The Jewish communities in Ethiopia viewed the seven days of Passover as a full week, or as a single Sabbath, in the language of the Torah, and thus held that one ought to count seven further Sabbaths (i.e., weeks) from the day following the seventh day of the Passover holiday, and then celebrate Pentecost on the fiftieth day. Consequently, the counting of the Omer was started on the 22nd day of Nisan, and the holiday of Shavuot was observed on the 12th of Sivan.

SEARCH FOR ḤAMETZ

On the night before Pesaḥ (Thursday night if Pesaḥ falls on Motza'ei Shabbat), a search for ḥametz is made in the house, customarily by candlelight. Before beginning the search, make the following blessing:

Blessed are You, LORD our God, King of the Universe,
who has made us holy through His commandments,
and has commanded us about the removal of leaven.

After the search, say:
May all ḥametz or leaven that is in my possession
which I have not seen or removed
be annulled and deemed like the dust of the earth.

On the following morning, after burning the ḥametz, say:
May all ḥametz or leaven that is in my possession,
whether I have seen it or not, whether I have removed it or not,
be annulled and deemed like the dust of the earth.

EIRUV TAVSHILIN

It is not permitted to cook for Shabbat when a Yom Tov falls on Thursday or Friday unless an Eiruv Tavshilin has been made prior to the Yom Tov. This is done by taking a piece of matza together with a boiled egg or some cooked food to be used on Shabbat. While holding them, say the following:

Blessed are You, LORD our God, King of the Universe,
who has made us holy through His commandments,
and has commanded us about the mitzva of Eruv.

By this Eruv may we be permitted to bake, cook, insulate food,
light a flame and do everything necessary on the festival
for the sake of the Sabbath, for us and for all Jews living in this city.

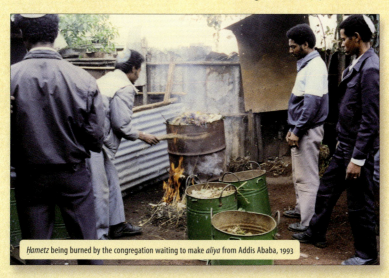

Ḥametz being burned by the congregation waiting to make *aliya* from Addis Ababa, 1993

ביעור חמץ

אור לארבעה עשר ניסן (ואם חל בשבת – אור לשלושה עשר) בודקין את החמץ לאור הנר.
לפני הבדיקה מברכים:

בָּרוּךְ אַתָּה יהוה אֱלֹהֵינוּ מֶלֶךְ הָעוֹלָם
אֲשֶׁר קִדְּשָׁנוּ בְּמִצְוֹתָיו וְצִוָּנוּ עַל בִּעוּר חָמֵץ.

אחר הבדיקה אומרים:

כָּל חֲמִירָא וַחֲמִיעָא דְּאִכָּא בִּרְשׁוּתִי
דְּלָא חֲמִתֵּהּ וּדְלָא בְעַרְתֵּהּ
לִבְטִיל וְלֶהֱוֵי הֶפְקֵר כְּעַפְרָא דְאַרְעָא.

ערב פסח שחרית, בשעה החמישית של היום, שורפים את החמץ ואחר כך אומרים:

כָּל חֲמִירָא וַחֲמִיעָא דְּאִכָּא בִּרְשׁוּתִי
דַּחֲמִתֵּהּ וּדְלָא חֲמִתֵּהּ, דְּבִעַרְתֵּהּ וּדְלָא בְעַרְתֵּהּ
לִבְטִיל וְלֶהֱוֵי הֶפְקֵר כְּעַפְרָא דְאַרְעָא.

עירוב תבשילין

בחוץ לארץ, אם חל ערב פסח ביום הרביעי, עושים עירוב תבשילין.
נוטלים מצה ותבשיל ואומרים:

בָּרוּךְ אַתָּה יהוה אֱלֹהֵינוּ מֶלֶךְ הָעוֹלָם
אֲשֶׁר קִדְּשָׁנוּ בְּמִצְוֹתָיו וְצִוָּנוּ עַל מִצְוַת עֵרוּב.

בְּדֵן עֵרוּבָא יְהֵא שָׁרֵא לָנָא לְמֵיפָא וּלְבַשָּׁלָא
וּלְאַטְמָנָא וּלְאַדְלָקָא שְׁרָגָא וּלְמֶעְבַּד כָּל צָרְכָּנָא
מִיּוֹמָא טָבָא לְשַׁבְּתָא
לָנוּ וּלְכָל יִשְׂרָאֵל הַדָּרִים בָּעִיר הַזֹּאת.

25

NISAN HALLELUYA

Halleluya, Nisan, Nisan, Halleluya.

And the Lord said to Moses:

Go tell the children of Israel

And say to the House of Jacob:

In the first month, that very month

I did redeem you from the land of Egypt.

It shall be the first month of the year

And His name shall be blessed on the first
day of the new month.

(*And You Shall Tell Your Children, 9*)

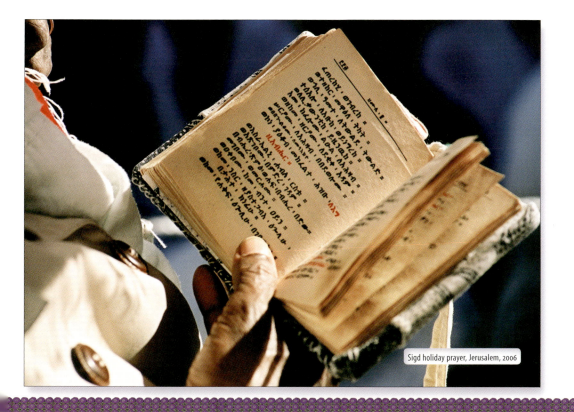

Sigd holiday prayer, Jerusalem, 2006

הדלקת נרות

בָּרוּךְ אַתָּה יהוה אֱלֹהֵינוּ מֶלֶךְ הָעוֹלָם
אֲשֶׁר קִדְּשָׁנוּ בְּמִצְוֹתָיו
וְצִוָּנוּ לְהַדְלִיק נֵר שֶׁל (שַׁבָּת וְשֶׁל) יוֹם טוֹב.

בָּרוּךְ אַתָּה יהוה אֱלֹהֵינוּ מֶלֶךְ הָעוֹלָם
שֶׁהֶחֱיָנוּ וְקִיְּמָנוּ, וְהִגִּיעָנוּ לַזְּמַן הַזֶּה.

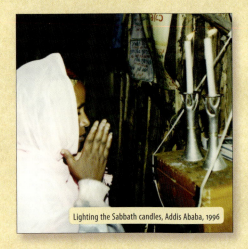

Lighting the Sabbath candles, Addis Ababa, 1996

CANDLE LIGHTING

Blessed are You, Lord our God, King of the Universe,
who has made us holy through His commandments,
and has commanded us to light
(the Sabbath light and) the festival light.

Blessed are You, Lord our God, King of the Universe,
who has given us life, sustained us, and brought us to this time.

The Seder Plate

Three Matzot are placed before the Leader of the Seder, along with the Seder Plate, which contains the following items:

እንቁላል
ביצה
THE EGG

ቅልጥም
זרוע
THE SHANK BONE

መራራ ቅጠል
מרור
THE BITTER HERBS

አረንጓዴ ቅጠል
כרפס
THE KARPAS

ሀሮሴት
חרוסת
THE ḤAROSET

ሀዘፈት
חזרת
THE MARROR FOR THE SANDWICH

The program for the evening is announced
beforehand in the following form:

Kiddush	መቀደስ	קדש
Washing The Hands	መታጠብ	ורחץ
Karpas	አረንጓዴ ቅጠል	כרפס
Dividing The Matza	መቁረስ	יחץ
Telling The Story	መተረክ	מגיד
Washing The Hands	መታጠብ	רחצה
Blessing Over Matza	ቂጣ ማውጣት	מוציא מצה
Eating The Bitter Herb	መራራ ቅጠል	מרור
The Bitter Sandwich	መጠቅለል	כורך
The Festive Meal	ማዕድ	שלחן עורך
Eating The Afikoman	ድብቅ	צפון
Grace After Meals	መባረክ	ברך
Hallel	ማወደስ	הלל
Conclusion	ተፈጸመ	נרצה

KIDDUSH

The first cup of wine is poured. Lift the cup with the right hand and say the following (on Shabbat, add the words in parentheses):

I am hereby prepared and ready to fulfill the commandment of the first of the four cups. For the sake of the unification of the Holy One, blessed be He, and His Divine Presence, through that which is hidden and concealed, in the name of all Israel.

(*Quietly:* And there was evening and there was morning – the sixth day. And the heavens and the earth were finished, and all their host. And by the seventh day God ended His work which He had done; and He rested on the seventh day from all His work which He had done. And God blessed the seventh day and sanctified it, because on it He rested from all His work which God had created and done.)

Blessed are You,
LORD our God, King of the Universe,
who creates the produce of the vine.

who has chosen us from among all peoples, raised us above all tongues, and made us holy through His commandments. You have given us, LORD our God, in love (Sabbaths for rest), festivals for rejoicing, holy days and seasons for joy, (this Sabbath day and) the festival of Matzot, the time of our freedom, (with love) a holy assembly in memory

of the exodus from Egypt. For You have chosen
us and sanctifed us above all peoples,
and given us as our heritage
(Your holy Sabbath
in love and favor and)
Your holy festivals
for joy and gladness.
Blessed are You, O LORD,
who sanctifies (the Sabbath,) Israel and the festivals.

30

מוזגים כוס ראשון, נוטלו ביד ימינו ומקדש:

הנני מוכן ומזומן לקיים מצוות כוס ראשון של ארבע כוסות.
לשם ייחוד קודשא בריך הוא ושכינתיה על ידי ההוא טמיר ונעלם בשם כל ישראל.

(בלחש: וַיְהִי־עֶרֶב וַיְהִי־בֹקֶר
יוֹם הַשִׁשִּׁי: וַיְכֻלּוּ הַשָׁמַיִם וְהָאָרֶץ וְכָל־צְבָאָם: וַיְכַל אֱלֹהִים בַּיּוֹם הַשְׁבִיעִי
מְלַאכְתּוֹ אֲשֶׁר עָשָׂה, וַיִּשְׁבֹּת בַּיּוֹם הַשְׁבִיעִי מִכָּל־מְלַאכְתּוֹ אֲשֶׁר עָשָׂה: וַיְבָרֶךְ
אֱלֹהִים אֶת־יוֹם הַשְׁבִיעִי, וַיְקַדֵּשׁ אֹתוֹ, כִּי בוֹ שָׁבַת מִכָּל־מְלַאכְתּוֹ, אֲשֶׁר־בָּרָא
אֱלֹהִים, לַעֲשׂוֹת.)

סברי מרנן

בָּרוּךְ אַתָּה יהוה אֱלֹהֵינוּ מֶלֶךְ הָעוֹלָם, בּוֹרֵא פְּרִי הַגָּפֶן.

בָּרוּךְ אַתָּה יהוה אֱלֹהֵינוּ מֶלֶךְ הָעוֹלָם, אֲשֶׁר בָּחַר
בָּנוּ מִכָּל עָם, וְרוֹמְמָנוּ מִכָּל לָשׁוֹן, וְקִדְּשָׁנוּ בְּמִצְוֹתָיו
וַתִּתֶּן לָנוּ יהוה אֱלֹהֵינוּ בְּאַהֲבָה (שַׁבָּתוֹת לִמְנוּחָה
וּ)מוֹעֲדִים לְשִׂמְחָה, חַגִּים וּזְמַנִּים לְשָׂשׂוֹן, אֶת
יוֹם (הַשַׁבָּת הַזֶּה וְאֶת יוֹם) חַג הַמַּצוֹת הַזֶּה
זְמַן חֵרוּתֵנוּ (בְּאַהֲבָה) מִקְרָא קֹדֶשׁ
זֵכֶר לִיצִיאַת מִצְרָיִם, כִּי בָנוּ
בָחַרְתָּ וְאוֹתָנוּ קִדַּשְׁתָּ
מִכָּל הָעַמִּים, (וְשַׁבָּת)
וּמוֹעֲדֵי קָדְשֶׁךָ
(בְּאַהֲבָה וּבְרָצוֹן)
בְּשִׂמְחָה וּבְשָׂשׂוֹן הִנְחַלְתָּנוּ.
בָּרוּךְ אַתָּה יהוה, מְקַדֵּשׁ (הַשַׁבָּת וְ)יִשְׂרָאֵל וְהַזְּמַנִּים.

בָּרוּךְ אַתָּה יהוה אֱלֹהֵינוּ מֶלֶךְ הָעוֹלָם, בּוֹרֵא מְאוֹרֵי הָאֵשׁ.

בָּרוּךְ אַתָּה יהוה אֱלֹהֵינוּ מֶלֶךְ הָעוֹלָם

הַמַּבְדִּיל בֵּין קֹדֶשׁ לְחֹל

בֵּין אוֹר לְחֹשֶׁךְ

בֵּין יִשְׂרָאֵל לָעַמִּים

בֵּין יוֹם הַשְּׁבִיעִי לְשֵׁשֶׁת יְמֵי הַמַּעֲשֶׂה

בֵּין קְדֻשַּׁת שַׁבָּת לִקְדֻשַּׁת יוֹם טוֹב הִבְדַּלְתָּ

וְאֶת יוֹם הַשְּׁבִיעִי מִשֵּׁשֶׁת יְמֵי הַמַּעֲשֶׂה קִדַּשְׁתָּ

הִבְדַּלְתָּ וְקִדַּשְׁתָּ אֶת עַמְּךָ יִשְׂרָאֵל בִּקְדֻשָּׁתֶךָ.

בָּרוּךְ אַתָּה יהוה הַמַּבְדִּיל בֵּין קֹדֶשׁ לְקֹדֶשׁ.

בָּרוּךְ אַתָּה יהוה, אֱלֹהֵינוּ מֶלֶךְ הָעוֹלָם

שֶׁהֶחֱיָנוּ וְקִיְּמָנוּ וְהִגִּיעָנוּ לַזְּמַן הַזֶּה.

שׁוֹתִים בַּהֲסִבַּת שְׂמֹאל.

On Motza'ei Shabbat, add the following:

> Blessed are You, Lord our God,
> King of the Universe, who creates the light of the fire.

Blessed are You, Lord our God, King of the Universe, who creates the light of the fire. Blessed are You, Lord our God, King of the Universe, who distinguishes between sacred and secular, between light and darkness, between Israel and the nations, between the seventh day and the six days of work. You have made a distinction between the holiness of the Sabbath and the holiness of festivals, and have sanctifed the seventh day above the six days of work. You have distinguished and sanctifed Your people Israel with Your holiness. Blessed are You, Lord, who distinguishes between sacred and sacred. Blessed are You, O Lord, who makes distinction between holy and holy.

> Blessed are You, Lord our God, King of the Universe,
> who has given us life, sustained us, and brought us to this time.

Drink while reclining to the left.

32

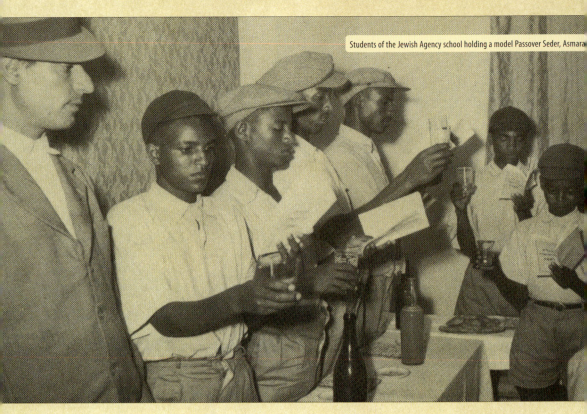

Students of the Jewish Agency school holding a model Passover Seder, Asmara

חחתאמ • ורחץ

מביאים לבעל הבית מים, נוטל ידיו ואינו מברך.

৫ঽঽৡ ৭ᠬᡏ • כרפס

נוטל מן הכרפס פחות מכזית, טובלו במי מלח או בחומץ ומברך
(מכוון לפטור בברכה זו גם את המרור):

בָּרוּךְ אַתָּה יהוה, אֱלֹהֵינוּ מֶלֶךְ הָעוֹלָם
בּוֹרֵא פְּרִי הָאֲדָמָה.

אוכלים בלי הסבה.

WASHING THE HANDS

The participants wash their hands but do not say a blessing.

KARPAS

A small quantity of radish, greens, or roots of parsley is dipped in salt water.
Say the following over the karpas, with the intent
to include the maror in the blessing:

Blessed are You, LORD our God, King of the Universe,
who creates the produce of the soil.

Eat without reclining.

DIVIDING THE MATZA

The middle matza is broken in two. The bigger portion is then hidden away to serve as the Afikoman with which the meal is later concluded. The smaller portion is placed between the two whole matzot.

wheat for the preparation of matza, Wolleka, 1984

הגדה • **מַגִּיד** מגלה את המצות, מגביה את הקערה, ואומר:

הנני מוכן ומזומן לקיים המצווה לספר ביציאת מצרים.
לשם ייחוד קודשא בריך הוא ושכינתיה על ידי ההוא טמיר ונעלם בשם כל ישראל.

TELLING THE STORY

*The matzot are uncovered and
the ke'ara (ritual dish) is held up.*

הָא
לַחְמָא עַנְיָא
דִּי אֲכָלוּ אֲבָהָתָנָא בְּאַרְעָא דְמִצְרָיִם
כָּל דִּכְפִין יֵיתֵי וְיֵכֹל, כָּל דִּצְרִיךְ יֵיתֵי וְיִפְסַח
הָשַׁתָּא הָכָא   לְשָׁנָה הַבָּאָה בְּאַרְעָא דְיִשְׂרָאֵל
הָשַׁתָּא עַבְדֵּי   לְשָׁנָה הַבָּאָה בְּנֵי חוֹרִין.

THIS
IS THE BREAD OF AFFLICTION

which our fathers did eat in the land of Egypt.
Let all who hunger come and eat.
Let all who are in need come and partake of the Pesaḥ lamb!
This year we are here;
Next year – in the land of Israel!
This year we are slaves;
Next year – free men!

Passover, Wolleka, 1984

How Our Forefathers Found Their Way to Ethiopia

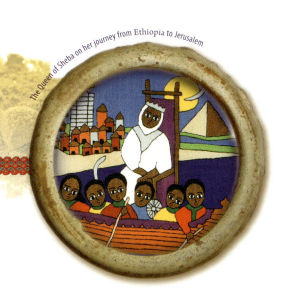

During the period of the First Temple, in the days of Sennacherib, King of Assyria, and Nebuchadnezzar, King of Babylon, many captives were taken from the land of Israel and exiled to Egypt. In the year 3203 since the creation of the world, our forefathers were exiled from Jerusalem to Egypt.

About 150 years after Zion was captured by Babylon, Alexander the Great conquered the entire area, including Egypt. He destroyed the gods of Egypt but did not damage the temple that the Jews had erected in the country.

The Egyptians rose up against the Jews and waged war against them, since they suspected that the Jews had collaborated with the Greeks. The Jews were defeated and exiled once more, heading south along the Nile until they reached Sudan. This was 410 years before the Christian calendar began.

They continued their journey from the city of Khartoum in Sudan, walking along the Blue Nile in a southeasterly direction. They then proceeded along the Guang River, which begins in the Chilga mountain ranges of Ethiopia near Gondar and flows westward. They entered Ethiopia through the Quara region which connects Sudan to the northwestern border of Ethiopia, and from there they pressed onwards into the districts around Lake Tana, making their way into the Gondar region, along the Semien Mountains until finally they reached Tigray.

When the Jews arrived in Ethiopia, they found the locals to be out of touch with the ways and wisdom of the times, and they influenced the natives to follow their faith in the God of Israel.

Oral tradition as related by the priests of the community (M.W.A.)

Africa – Münster Map, 1544

מוזגים כוס שני ומסלקים (או מכסים) את הקערה.
הבן שואל:

מַה נִּשְׁתַּנָּה

הַלַּיְלָה הַזֶּה מִכָּל הַלֵּילוֹת

שֶׁבְּכָל הַלֵּילוֹת אָנוּ אוֹכְלִין חָמֵץ וּמַצָּה
הַלַּיְלָה הַזֶּה כֻּלּוֹ מַצָּה

שֶׁבְּכָל הַלֵּילוֹת אָנוּ אוֹכְלִין שְׁאָר יְרָקוֹת
הַלַּיְלָה הַזֶּה מָרוֹר

שֶׁבְּכָל הַלֵּילוֹת אֵין אָנוּ מַטְבִּילִין אֲפִלּוּ פַּעַם אֶחָת
הַלַּיְלָה הַזֶּה שְׁתֵּי פְעָמִים

שֶׁבְּכָל הַלֵּילוֹת אָנוּ אוֹכְלִין בֵּין יוֹשְׁבִין וּבֵין מְסֻבִּין
הַלַּיְלָה הַזֶּה כֻּלָּנוּ מְסֻבִּין

The ke'ara is removed (or covered) and the second cup of wine is poured.
The youngest child asks the following questions:

HOW DIFFERENT

IS THIS NIGHT FROM ALL OTHER NIGHTS

On all other nights we may eat either ḥametz or matza;
why on this night only matza?

On all other nights we eat other kinds of herbs;
why on this night bitter herbs?

On all other nights we do not even dip the herbs once;
why on this night do we dip twice?

On all other nights we eat either sitting or reclining;
why on this night do we all recline?

Seder night, Addis Ababa, 1999

Feminine Fortitude

RECOLLECTIONS OF KING SARSA DENGEL (1597–1563)

And the war raged between the Falashas and the soldiers of the King...

This time, half the Falashas fell before the spear and the other half lost their lives in the valley as they tried to escape. Even the animals, including the oxen, camels, donkeys and mules, were killed – not a single one was left alive as they destroyed them all...

An amazing occurrence took place at this time, involving a woman who had been taken captive and was being led by her captor with her hands bound to his. When she saw that they were walking along the edge of a rather large valley, she cried out: "Lord help me!" – and she threw herself into the valley, dragging along with her the man who had tied her hands unwillingly to his own.

How astounding is the fortitude of this woman, who was willing to sacrifice her own life rather than be held captive by the Christian community! And while it is true that she was not alone in her actions and many other women acted as she did, yet she was the first one whose actions I witnessed with my very own eyes.

The behavior of these women is very similar to that of the forty men under the command of Ben-Gurion who swore to accept death by killing one another rather than giving themselves up to the ruling Romans, and they all died on that very day. Only Joseph was saved through his intelligence. In this way, the death of our ancestors was repeated by that of our present-day martyrs, for they chose death over becoming subservient to people who did not practice the same faith. For Jews can never worship as the Christians in any way, shape or form...

(Halévy, *Sarsa Dengel*, 263–267)

Prayer, Gondar, 2008

עֲבָדִים הָיִינוּ

לְפַרְעֹה בְּמִצְרָיִם

וַיּוֹצִיאֵנוּ יהוה אֱלֹהֵינוּ מִשָּׁם

בְּיָד חֲזָקָה וּבִזְרוֹעַ נְטוּיָה.

וְאִלּוּ לֹא הוֹצִיא הַקָּדוֹשׁ בָּרוּךְ הוּא

אֶת אֲבוֹתֵינוּ מִמִּצְרַיִם

הֲרֵי אָנוּ וּבָנֵינוּ וּבְנֵי בָנֵינוּ מְשֻׁעְבָּדִים הָיִינוּ

לְפַרְעֹה בְּמִצְרָיִם.

וַאֲפִלוּ

כֻּלָּנוּ חֲכָמִים, כֻּלָּנוּ נְבוֹנִים, כֻּלָּנוּ זְקֵנִים

כֻּלָּנוּ יוֹדְעִים אֶת הַתּוֹרָה

מִצְוָה עָלֵינוּ לְסַפֵּר בִּיצִיאַת מִצְרָיִם

וְכָל הַמַּרְבֶּה לְסַפֵּר בִּיצִיאַת מִצְרָיִם

הֲרֵי זֶה מְשֻׁבָּח.

*The ke'ara is returned to its place
and the matzot uncovered.*

SLAVES WE WERE

to Pharaoh in Egypt
But the Lord our God brought us out of there
with a strong hand and an outstretched arm.
And if the Holy One, blessed is He,
had not brought our fathers out from Egypt,
then we, and our children
and our children's children
would still be slaves to Pharaoh in Egypt.
Now even if
we were all wise, even if we were all clever,
even if we were all old,
and even if we were all learned in the Torah,
it would still be our duty to tell the story
of the going out of Egypt.
And the more one dwells on the story
of the going out of Egypt,
the more praise one deserves.

Has the Time Come to Return to the Holy Land?

Ethiopia 5622 (1862)

Blessed be the Lord of Israel, the God of all flesh and spirits.

I would like the present missive, which is being sent by Abba Tzega, be delivered to the priest in Jerusalem known as Kacha [?] Joseph, the high priest of all Jews.

I hope that this letter reaches you through Birnchusa [a corruption of the name Bronkhorst – Ed].

My Jewish brethren, peace be with you. We sent an earlier letter to you with Daniel the son Ḥanania, the father of Moses.

We are writing to inquire whether the time has come for us to return again to our land, that is, the Holy Land, and to Jerusalem, the holy city. For we are a destitute nation and we have neither a judge nor a prophet in our midst. If the time has truly come, please send us a letter regarding this matter. For you are indeed superior to us, and we look to you for guidance during these times. A great wind is stirring in our souls now, and there are those who are saying that the time has come for us to separate ourselves from the Christians and travel to your city of Jerusalem to reunite with our brethren and offer sacrifices to the Lord, God of Israel, in the Holy Land.

We thus commission you, Birnchusa, on the basis of the love that you have shown us in the past, to deliver a response to us from our distant brethren.

May you go and come in peace, and may peace always reign over our brethren in the Holy Land, which the Lord gave to his servant Moses as he stood on Mount Sinai.

I, Abba Tzega, community elder and leader, do hereby send you this present missive in the second month of the year 7354 after creation.

(Waldman, *Beyond*, 127–128)

Community priests in the synagogue, Ambover, 1983

מַעֲשֶׂה

בְּרַבִּי אֱלִיעֶזֶר וְרַבִּי יְהוֹשֻׁעַ וְרַבִּי אֶלְעָזָר בֶּן עֲזַרְיָה

וְרַבִּי עֲקִיבָא וְרַבִּי טַרְפוֹן

שֶׁהָיוּ מְסֻבִּין בִּבְנֵי בְרַק

וְהָיוּ מְסַפְּרִים בִּיצִיאַת מִצְרַיִם כָּל אוֹתוֹ הַלַּיְלָה

עַד שֶׁבָּאוּ תַלְמִידֵיהֶם וְאָמְרוּ לָהֶם

רַבּוֹתֵינוּ, הִגִּיעַ זְמַן קְרִיאַת שְׁמַע שֶׁל שַׁחֲרִית.

אָמַר רַבִּי אֶלְעָזָר בֶּן עֲזַרְיָה

הֲרֵי אֲנִי כְּבֶן שִׁבְעִים שָׁנָה

וְלֹא זָכִיתִי שֶׁתֵּאָמֵר יְצִיאַת מִצְרַיִם בַּלֵּילוֹת

עַד שֶׁדְּרָשָׁהּ בֶּן זוֹמָא

שֶׁנֶּאֱמַר

לְמַעַן תִּזְכֹּר אֶת־יוֹם צֵאתְךָ מֵאֶרֶץ מִצְרַיִם

כֹּל יְמֵי חַיֶּיךָ:

A TALE

of Rabbi Eliezer, and Rabbi Yehoshua,
and Rabbi Elazar son of Azarya,
and Rabbi Akiva, and Rabbi Tarfon,
who were reclining at the Seder service
in Benei Berak,
and had spent the whole night long
telling the story of the going out of Egypt,
until their pupils came and said to them:
"Our masters,
it is time to recite the morning Shema!"

יְמֵי חַיֶּיךָ	הַיָּמִים
כֹּל יְמֵי חַיֶּיךָ	הַלֵּילוֹת.

וַחֲכָמִים אוֹמְרִים

Said Rabbi Elazar son of Azarya,
"Now I am like a man of seventy,
but I had never yet understood
why the going out from Egypt
should be mentioned at nighttime,
until Ben Zoma explained it to me from the verse,
'That you may remember the day
when you came out of Egypt
all the days of your life.'

יְמֵי חַיֶּיךָ	הָעוֹלָם הַזֶּה
כֹּל יְמֵי חַיֶּיךָ	לְהָבִיא לִימוֹת הַמָּשִׁיחַ.

| 'The days of your life,' | means, | just the days! |
| But 'all the days of your life,' | means, | the nights as well! |

But the sages explain:

| 'The days of your life,' | means, | this life! |
| But 'All the days of your life,' | means, | the days of the Messiah as well!" |

בָּרוּךְ הַמָּקוֹם
בָּרוּךְ הוּא
בָּרוּךְ שֶׁנָּתַן תּוֹרָה לְעַמּוֹ יִשְׂרָאֵל
בָּרוּךְ הוּא

BLESSED IS THE ALL-PRESENT GOD,
BLESSED IS HE,
BLESSED IS HE WHO GAVE THE TORAH
TO HIS PEOPLE ISRAEL,
BLESSED IS HE.

community priest with a Torah scroll, Uzava 1958

כְּנֶגֶד
אַרְבָּעָה בָּנִים דִּבְּרָה תוֹרָה

אֶחָד
חָכָם

וְאֶחָד
רָשָׁע

וְאֶחָד
תָּם

וְאֶחָד
שֶׁאֵינוֹ יוֹדֵעַ לִשְׁאֹל

THE TORAH, IN VARIOUS PLACES,
ALLUDES TO FOUR TYPES OF CHILDREN

ONE
WISE

ONE
WICKED

ONE
SIMPLE

ONE
**TOO SMALL
TO ASK A QUESTION**

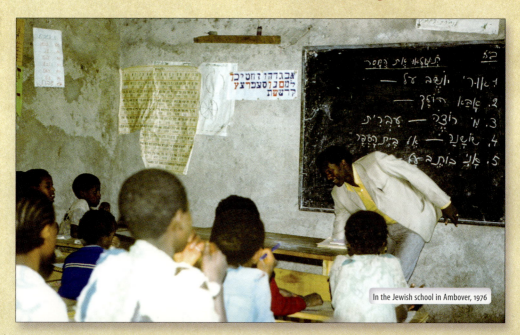

In the Jewish school in Ambover, 1976

חָכָם

מַה הוּא אוֹמֵר

מָה הָעֵדֹת וְהַחֻקִּים וְהַמִּשְׁפָּטִים
אֲשֶׁר צִוָּה יהוה אֱלֹהֵינוּ אֶתְכֶם:
וְאַף אַתָּה אֱמָר לוֹ כְּהִלְכוֹת הַפֶּסַח
אֵין מַפְטִירִין אַחַר הַפֶּסַח אֲפִיקוֹמָן.

What does the
WISE
child say?

"What mean the testimonies, and the statutes,
and the judgments,
which the LORD our God has commanded you?"
You too must tell him all the detailed regulations
of the Pesaḥ,
for instance, that we do not proceed to any dessert
after eating the Pesaḥ lamb.

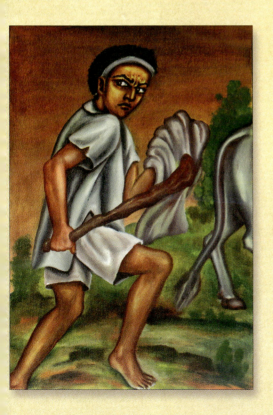

רָשָׁע

מַה הוּא אוֹמֵר

מָה הָעֲבֹדָה הַזֹּאת לָכֶם:

לָכֶם וְלֹא לוֹ

וּלְפִי שֶׁהוֹצִיא אֶת עַצְמוֹ מִן הַכְּלָל

כָּפַר בָּעִקָּר

וְאַף אַתָּה הַקְהֵה אֶת שִׁנָּיו, וֶאֱמָר לוֹ

בַּעֲבוּר זֶה עָשָׂה יהוה לִי בְּצֵאתִי מִמִּצְרָיִם:

לִי וְלֹא לוֹ

אִלּוּ הָיָה שָׁם, לֹא הָיָה נִגְאָל.

What does the

WICKED

child say?

"What mean you by this service?"

meaning you and not himself –

and since he excludes himself from the company,

showing that he rejects

the main principle of the Pesaḥ,

you should also make him feel uncomfortable

by quoting:

"This is done because of that which the LORD did for me

when I came out of Egypt!"

ME and not HIM!

Because if he had been there, he would not have been saved.

תָּם

מַה הוּא אוֹמֵר
מַה־זֹּאת
וְאָמַרְתָּ אֵלָיו
בְּחֹזֶק יָד הוֹצִיאָנוּ יהוה
מִמִּצְרַיִם מִבֵּית עֲבָדִים:

What does the
SIMPLE
child ask?
"What is this?"
And you shall say to him,
"By strength of hand the LORD
brought us out of Egypt,
out of the house of bondage."

וְשֶׁאֵינוֹ יוֹדֵעַ לִשְׁאֹל

אַתְּ פְּתַח לוֹ
שֶׁנֶּאֱמַר
וְהִגַּדְתָּ לְבִנְךָ בַּיּוֹם הַהוּא לֵאמֹר
בַּעֲבוּר זֶה עָשָׂה יהוה לִי בְּצֵאתִי מִמִּצְרָיִם:

And as for the child who is

TO SMALL TO ASK A QUESTION

you should prompt him,
as it is said:
"And you shall tell your son on that day, saying,
This is because of what the Lord did for me
when I came out of Egypt."

Attempts to Make Aliya to the Land of Israel

Community priests in front of the synagogue in Ambover, 1971(?)

5622 (1862)

In the days of King Tewodros II (1855–1868), there was a widespread belief throughout the Beta Israel community that the Messiah was about to arrive. According to their belief, the name of the Messiah would be Tewodros, meaning "the gift of God."

These were difficult times for the Jews. The King constantly persecuted and oppressed them. This period is known in Amharic as *kefu zemen*, the "Time of Evil."

Many Jews considered making *aliya* to the land of Israel. In the year 1862, a prophet rose up within the Beta Israel community. There are those who say that his name was Abba Sirak, while others claim that his name was Pinkhas.

The prophet proclaimed: "God appeared to me in a dream and said: 'I do solemnly promise that in a short while I will redeem my people from Ethiopia just as I redeemed them from Egypt. Just as Moses led the children of Israel out of Egypt, so Abba Mehari will lead you out of Ethiopia. I have chosen Abba Mehari as your leader.'"

Abba Mehari believed that the hour of redemption had arrived and he therefore asked all the Jews to join him and undertake the journey to the land of Israel. Hundreds and thousands of Jews came from all the villages to join him. They came from all the different regions of the country, such as Semien, Dembiya, Sekelt. They sold off all their possessions and prepared themselves for the journey.

However, the road was more difficult than they had anticipated. They did not experience any miracles. The people were hungry and did not know the way all that well. They arrived at the banks of the Red Sea. There they expected that the waters would part before them and they would cross the sea on dry land just as had happened in the days of Moses, but these expectations proved to be false.

Twelve priests jumped into the sea and began to swim, but the waters still did not part. The priests grew tired and returned to dry land.

The Jews were despondent and their spirits were quite low. They began to return southward, to the homes that they had left behind. They were tired and hungry, sick and weak. Many died along the way and were buried in the region of Tigray. Some of them remained in the Shire region. Only a handful managed to return safely to their villages of origin. They did not forget the land of Israel and did not cease to dream of Jerusalem. They continued to pray and believe that one day the final redemption would come.

(*Tales*, 36–37)

(וְהִגַּדְתָּ לְבִנְךָ)
יָכוֹל מֵראֹשׁ חֹדֶשׁ
תַּלְמוּד לוֹמַר:
(בַּיּוֹם הַהוּא.)
אִי בַּיּוֹם הַהוּא
יָכוֹל מִבְּעוֹד יוֹם
תַּלְמוּד לוֹמַר:
(בַּעֲבוּר זֶה.)
בַּעֲבוּר זֶה לֹא אָמַרְתִּי
אֶלָּא בְּשָׁעָה שֶׁיֵּשׁ
מַצָּה וּמָרוֹר מֻנָּחִים לְפָנֶיךָ.

("And you shall tell your son")
this could mean
you should begin to tell the story at New Moon.
So the verse adds, "on that day."
Now if it says, ("on that day,") it could mean
that we start in the daytime.
So the verse adds, ("Because of this";)
"Because of this" means –
only when the matza and maror are laid before you.

מִתְּחִלָּה

עוֹבְדֵי עֲבוֹדָה זָרָה הָיוּ אֲבוֹתֵינוּ

AT THE BEGINNING

**OUR FATHERS
WERE IDOL WORSHIPERS,**

וְעַכְשָׁו

קֵרְבָנוּ הַמָּקוֹם לַעֲבוֹדָתוֹ

BUT NOW

**GOD HAS BROUGHT US NEAR
TO SERVE HIM,**

as it is said:

"And Joshua said to all the people,
Thus says the LORD God of Israel,
Your fathers dwelt
on the other side of the river in ancient times:
Terah was the father of Abraham,
and the father of Naḥor:
and they served other gods.
And I took your father Abraham
from the other side of the river,
and led him through all the land of Kena'an,
and multiplied his seed,
and gave him Isaac.
And I gave to Isaac, Jacob and Esau,
and I gave to Esau Mount Se'ir to possess it;

**BUT JACOB AND HIS CHILDREN
WENT DOWN INTO EGYPT."**

שֶׁנֶּאֱמַר

וַיֹּאמֶר יְהוֹשֻׁעַ אֶל־כָּל־הָעָם

כֹּה־אָמַר יהוה אֱלֹהֵי יִשְׂרָאֵל

בְּעֵבֶר הַנָּהָר יָשְׁבוּ אֲבוֹתֵיכֶם מֵעוֹלָם

תֶּרַח אֲבִי אַבְרָהָם וַאֲבִי נָחוֹר

וַיַּעַבְדוּ אֱלֹהִים אֲחֵרִים:

וָאֶקַּח אֶת־אֲבִיכֶם אֶת־אַבְרָהָם מֵעֵבֶר הַנָּהָר

וָאוֹלֵךְ אוֹתוֹ בְּכָל־אֶרֶץ כְּנָעַן

וָאַרְבֶּה אֶת־זַרְעוֹ, וָאֶתֶּן־לוֹ אֶת־יִצְחָק:

וָאֶתֵּן לְיִצְחָק אֶת־יַעֲקֹב וְאֶת־עֵשָׂו

וָאֶתֵּן לְעֵשָׂו אֶת־הַר שֵׂעִיר לָרֶשֶׁת אוֹתוֹ

וְיַעֲקֹב וּבָנָיו יָרְדוּ מִצְרָיִם:

50

WE CAME FROM THE WEST
AND FROM THE WEST
WE SHALL RETURN

It is an ancient tradition that the Jews first entered Ethiopia from the west, through Sudan. It is along that very same path – in the west, through Sudan – that the Jews of Ethiopia will one day return to the land of Israel when the redemption comes.

Oral tradition as related by
community elders (M.W.A)

Making *aliya* to Israel, Operation Solomo

51

בָּרוּךְ שׁוֹמֵר הַבְטָחָתוֹ לְיִשְׂרָאֵל

בָּרוּךְ הוּא

שֶׁהַקָּדוֹשׁ בָּרוּךְ הוּא חִשַּׁב אֶת הַקֵּץ

לַעֲשׂוֹת כְּמָה שֶׁאָמַר לְאַבְרָהָם אָבִינוּ בִּבְרִית בֵּין הַבְּתָרִים

שֶׁנֶּאֱמַר

וַיֹּאמֶר לְאַבְרָם, יָדֹעַ תֵּדַע כִּי־גֵר יִהְיֶה זַרְעֲךָ בְּאֶרֶץ לֹא לָהֶם

וַעֲבָדוּם וְעִנּוּ אֹתָם

אַרְבַּע מֵאוֹת שָׁנָה:

BLESSED IS THE ONE
WHO KEEPS HIS PROMISE TO ISRAEL,

וְגַם אֶת־הַגּוֹי אֲשֶׁר יַעֲבֹדוּ דָּן אָנֹכִי

וְאַחֲרֵי־כֵן יֵצְאוּ בִּרְכֻשׁ גָּדוֹל:

blessed is He.

For the Holy One, blessed is He,

had already worked out the end of their captivity,

in order to fulfill what He had said to our father Abraham

at the Covenant between the Pieces,

as it is said:

"And He said to Abram, Know surely that your seed

shall be strangers in a land that is not theirs,

and shall serve them;

and they shall afflict them for four hundred years;

and also that nation whom they shall serve, will I judge:

and afterwards they will come out
with great possessions."

◀ continue on page 58

The Vision of Abba Baruch

Abba Baruch, Amba Gualit, 1908

The Words of Abba Baruch Adhenen, one of the greatest Priests of Ethiopian Jewry, spoken before the priests and community elders after they asked him about the fate of Ethiopian Jewry, 5695 (1935).

If not now, then in a little while, be patient a while longer. When the time will come for your exodus it will be at sunset [in a time of great hardship – Ed.]. A leader will come to power who is not of royal lineage. In his time, the nation will experience much tragedy.

The Jews of Ethiopia will travel on foot towards Sudan and the ruling parties will capture them, put them in jail and torture them. But the powers that be shall not succeed in suppressing this awakening, which would be like trying to stop a flood with a mere dam, so our people will leave openly, and many shall die in Sudan – infants, as well as the young and old.

Those who will survive shall reach the land of Israel and enter homes that they did not build and take over vineyards that they did not plant; they shall eat and drink and be satisfied. Of those that remain in Ethiopia, some will make their way via the Red Sea, through Tigray. Many members of the nation, in making *aliya*, will find their food already prepared and their drinks already served, and the doors of the homes will be open before them. They will be told: "The time has come." Without even eating and drinking or closing up their homes, they will enter Jerusalem at a time of sunrise [days of plenty and blessing – Ed.].

The final *aliya* will come when the Seed of Israel will be sought out and they will be told that the moment has arrived for them to make *aliya*, and they shall indeed make *aliya*. At that time, religion in the land shall be like a tenuous cord but it shall not break. Whosoever shall pray during those times and cling to the Lord shall be saved.

During this time "old age will fall away like dry skin" [the elderly shall be rejuvenated – Ed.]. An elderly man of 80 shall become as one only 20 years old. Your joy shall be so great that you shall leap in the air, but you will take care not to trample too heavily upon the ground. Do not hate the land and say, "it is a shame that we came here," for the Lord does not appreciate such words.

When the time comes that all members of the people of Israel shall make their way to the land of Israel, there will be no rainfall in Ethiopia. Do not tell this to the ruling parties, for they shall refuse to let you make *aliya*.

(Ben Baruch Archives)

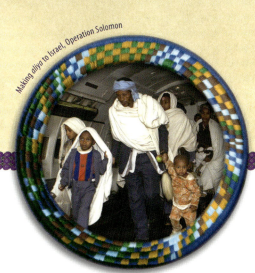

ACROSS THE RIVERS OF CUSH

And it shall come to pass in that day, that the Lord shall set His hand again the second time to recover the remnant of His people, that shall be left, from Assyria, and from Egypt, from Pathros, and from Cush, and from Eilam, and from Shinar, and from Ḥamat, and from the islands of the sea. And He shall set up a banner for the nations, and shall assemble the outcasts of Israel, and gather together the dispersed of Judah from the four corners of the earth.

Isaiah 11:11–12

From beyond the rivers of Cush come my suppliants, the scattered ones, who shall bring an offering to me.

Zephaniah 3:10

Navy boat off the coast of Sudan, 1981

Along the coast of Sudan, on the way to the ship named *Bat Galim*, 1981

O land of buzzing wings, which fly beyond the rivers of Cush: that sendest ambassadors by the sea, even in vessels of papyrus upon the waters: Go, swift messengers, to a nation tall and smooth, to a people terrible from their beginning onward; a nation mighty and conquering, whose land the rivers have divided! All you inhabitants of the world, and dwellers on the earth, see, when he lifts up a banner on the mountains; and when he blows a *shofar*, hear! For so the Lord said to me, I will take my rest, and I will look on in my dwelling place, like the clear heat in sunlight; and like the cloud of dew in the heat of harvest. For before the harvest, when the blossom is past, and the bud is ripening into young grapes, he shall both cut off the sprigs with pruning hooks, and take away and cut down the branches. They shall be left together to the predatory birds of the mountains, and to the beasts of the earth: and the birds shall summer upon them, and all the beasts of the earth shall winter upon them. In that name shall a present be brought to the Lord of hosts, by a people tall and smooth, even by a people terrible from their beginning onward; a nation mighty and conquering, whose land the rivers have divided, to the place of the name of the Lord of hosts, the Mount Zion.

Isaiah 18:1–7

Are there Also White Falashas Under the Sun?

Joseph Halévy, the first emissary sent to the Ethiopian Jewish community

Joseph Halévy, 5628 (1868)

When I arrived in the village I moved quickly and found a group of community members who had gathered in one of the village's central locations. The men, women and children, upon catching sight of me, cried out in amazement and terror at the sight of my skin and the nature of my clothing.

After the initial shock, a certain community elder approached me and asked me respectfully to withdraw from there and accompany him to a tent where a group of select individuals had congregated. As I approached the tent, the men rose and blessed me and surrounded me where they stood at a distance. When I attempted to approach them they all began to back away little by little, except for two of them who took my hands with love while the others called out to me in rather loud voices: "Atedresbeny!" (which means, "Don't touch us!").

In the meantime, an elderly man wearing a long coat came up to me and, after he had looked me over from head to toe, handed me a cup of water without saying a word. I was agitated and perturbed by the look in his eye, without understanding the meaning of this riddle, without any knowledge or comprehension of the thoughts going through the minds of these people. All the same I restrained myself in order to await the outcome of this strange unfolding of events…

Then I spoke up and said to them: "Hey! Beloved brethren, I am not a mere European, rather I am, like you, a child of Israel. I have not come from Europe merely in order to do business in the land of Cush, but to see how my brothers in this land fare, those who share the same faith as me. I have been sent to you by the leadership of Israelite brethren, which is a large and well-respected organization in my native land. Please know, my dear brothers, that I too am a member of the Falashas, and I am just like one of you! I do not believe in any god other than our Lord, and my religion is no different than the common religion we share and inherited as children of Israel at Mount Sinai!"

These words, which came from the depths of my heart, made a great impression on the Falashas. A few of them showed signs of joy at my words while others shook their heads and looked at one another as though they were unsure whether my words were actually spoken in good faith. In the end, many of them called out as one: "Behold, you are a Falasha! A Falasha with white skin! You mock us! Whoever heard of something like this or beheld it with his own eyes? Can it be that there are also white Falashas under the sun?"

I made an effort to explain to them and swear on my faith that all of the Falashas residing in Jerusalem and in the other countries in the world were all white and that there was no difference in skin color between them and the

nations in whose midst they made their homes. When the word Jerusalem left my lips, the atmosphere changed and all doubt was removed from the hearts of my listeners. Like a flash of lightning in the night, the name Jerusalem lit up the eyes and hearts of these lost brothers of ours. With tears in their eyes (tears of joy and longing) they called out as one: "Ah, have you too been to Jerusalem, the holy blessed city? Have you seen Mount Zion with your own eyes, that most beautiful of all mountains, and the house of the Lord, our Temple, towering on high with its sublime, esteemed sanctuary which the Lord God of Israel chose as the eternal dwelling for His splendid presence? Ah, have you seen with your own eyes the tomb of our foremother Rachel? Have you been to Bethlehem, and the city of Kiebron (Hebron) where our holy ancestors are buried?"

I had to make a great effort to answer all of their various questions, and they did not cease to bombard me with inquiries and shed tears at the memory of our sacred places from days of old.

These moments are precious to me and I shall not forget them for as long as I live, so long as the Lord gives me life. Lips of flesh and blood cannot suffice to paint an accurate picture of the emotions that stirred in my soul at that point, as I beheld the sublime image of the faces of my brethren, members of our same faith, black as a raven, with their shining eyes flashing from the force of their own emotions as they recalled the lofty exploits of our nation!

I related to them that before I had turned my steps towards the country of Cush, I had been in Jerusalem, and I informed them that this city, which had been the very epitome of beauty in days of old, had now lost its former glory and its gates had been destroyed. I told them that the place where our Temple had formerly stood, along with our splendid sanctuary, was now a house of prayer for the Ishmaelites.

When they heard these words they grew very sad and shed many tears until they no longer had strength to cry, and I wept along with them. These lost brothers of ours had believed that our Temple still stood in all its former glory and splendor and that the members of our nation who lived there were honored above all other nations. They had absolutely no knowledge of the state of the Holy Land at that point in time. They also had no idea that the Sultan now ruled over the country. A few of them related that they had a tradition in their community, handed down from generation to generation, that a great king in the West who belonged to the Christian tradition of the Romans still ruled over the Holy Land, and that the majority of the inhabitants were Jews who lived in great wealth and were greatly honored.

(Halévy, *Travel Letters*)

מכסה את המצות, אוחז את הכוס ואומר:

וְהִיא

שֶׁעָמְדָה לַאֲבוֹתֵינוּ וְלָנוּ

שֶׁלֹּא אֶחָד בִּלְבָד עָמַד עָלֵינוּ לְכַלּוֹתֵנוּ

אֶלָּא שֶׁבְּכָל דּוֹר וָדוֹר עוֹמְדִים עָלֵינוּ לְכַלּוֹתֵנוּ

וְהַקָּדוֹשׁ בָּרוּךְ הוּא מַצִּילֵנוּ מִיָּדָם

מניח את הכוס ומגלה את המצות.

The matzot are covered and the wine cup is raised.

AND THAT

promise to our fathers and ourselves has stood,
for not only one persecutor has risen to destroy us;
but in every generation
there are those who rise to destroy us.

BUT THE HOLY ONE,
BLESSED IS HE,
ALWAYS SAVES US FROM THEIR HANDS.

The wine cup is put down and the matzot are uncovered.

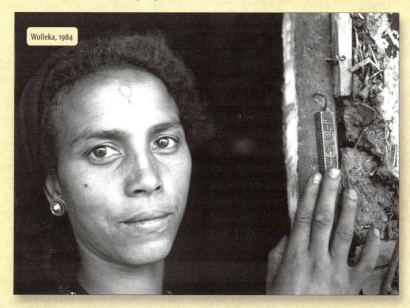

Wolleka, 1984

We, Like You, Believe in One God

Prayer on the Day of Remembrance for those lost in Sudan, Jerusalem, 2006

Gondar, 25th Nisan, 5663
(April 22, 1903)

Praised be the Lord God of Israel.

Shalom! Greetings! Peace be unto you in the land of Germany, you who live beyond the great sea, old and young alike! How does this letter find you?

We observe the laws of the Torah. Before we crossed the sea in the days of the kingdom of Solomon, we lived for forty years under the rule of Gideon.

We keep the commandments of Moses and continue to offer traditional sacrifices in accordance with the laws of Aaron. We are descendants of the tribe of Levi. We believe in a single God.

We were told: "Believe in the New Testament," but we preferred to lay down our lives rather than convert.

The ruler of Abyssinia supported us – may the Lord grant Menelik long life – however, since we left Jerusalem, we have been a poor people.

The sacrifice which we offer on the Passover holiday consists of a lamb and grain. This accords with the laws of the Torah as handed down to Aaron.

Shembera, Avimelech, Daniel and Mehari committed the present missive to writing. The letter should be distributed among all the Jews of Germany. We, like you, believe in one God.

(Waldman, *From Ethiopia*, 76)

Community priest before the entrance to the synagogue, Dembiya, 1908

O, Brothers, Do not Forget Us!

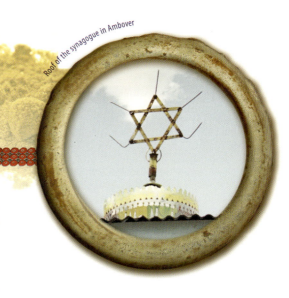

Roof of the synagogue in Ambover

Gurava Sekelt, 17th Adar II, 5665
(March 24, 1905)

Blessed is the Lord God of Israel.

The present letter has been sent from Abyssinia by the children of Israel known as Falashas to our brethren throughout the communities of Israel, the great sages of Jerusalem and other lands, and the congregations of Jews throughout the world.

Shalom! Greetings! Does this letter find you well?

In the days of the rulers Tewodros and Johannes, we were forcibly converted to Christianity. We chose death over conversion. The God of Abraham, Isaac and Jacob saved us. As a result of your prayers, a few of us survived. Previously we were rather great in number; in times past there were over two hundred synagogues. Today there are only thirty. In the time of the Dervishes many died of hunger. As a result of your prayers today we have a beneficent king. Menelik says: "Be like your forefathers!" May the Lord grant him long life!

However, the supporters of Flad who have overrun Abyssinia in its entirety these days, say: "Convert to Christianity," as they claim, "Whoever has not been baptized will be damned, and whoever has been baptized will be saved." But we shall fight for the Torah of Moses. On behalf of the Lord of Israel, please help us with your prayers.

The present letter was composed by the high priests Abba Aryen, Abba Tayem, and the scribe Debtera Teka, in the hope that it might make its way to the congregations of Israel, and the great sages through Yaakov the son of Moshe, who came to visit us.

We were truly happy to receive him; when a member of the people of Israel arrives here it is a cause for great joy.

Shalom, and may peace reign over you, children of Israel, our brethren who firmly protect the Torah of Moses.

O, brothers, do not forget us! We are desperate, our books have all been lost, the Dervishes destroyed them, burning them in their fires, and our schools have been razed to the ground. Please pray to the Lord on our behalf!

Written in Gurava Sekelt, on the 18th day of the 12th month.

(Waldman, *From Ethiopia*, 77–78)

Jacques Faitlovitch, Gondar, 1905

מַה בִּקֵּשׁ לָבָן הָאֲרַמִּי
לַעֲשׂוֹת לְיַעֲקֹב אָבִינוּ
שֶׁפַּרְעֹה לֹא גָזַר אֶלָּא עַל הַזְּכָרִים
וְלָבָן בִּקֵּשׁ לַעֲקֹר אֶת הַכֹּל

COME and LEARN

What Laban
the Aramean tried to do
to Jacob our father!
For Pharaoh decreed the death
of the male children only,
but Laban tried to exterminate us all –

as it is said,

'AN ARAMEAN SOUGHT TO DESTROY MY FATHER,
AND HE WENT DOWN TO EGYPT,

AND SOJOURNED THERE, WITH A FEW,

AND HE BECAME THERE A NATION, GREAT, MIGHTY,
AND POPULOUS.'

AND HE WENT DOWN TO MITZRAYIM

this means, forced by the divine Word;

AND SOJOURNED THERE

This means to teach us that our father Jacob
did not go down to settle in Egypt,
but only to stay for a time,
as it is written, 'And they said to Pharaoh,
to SOJOURN in the land are we come;
for thy servants have no pasture for their flocks;
for the famine is severe in the land of Caanan:
Now therefore, we pray thee,
let thy servants dwell in the land of Goshen.'

WITH A FEW

as it is said: "Your fathers went down to Egypt
with seventy persons,
and now the LORD your God has made you
like the stars of heaven for multitude."

AND HE BECAME THERE A NATION

this comes to teach that Israel
developed their distinctive ways there.

GREAT, MIGHTY

as it is said: "And the children of Israel were fruitful,
and increased abundantly.
and multiplied, and grew EXCEEDINGLY MIGHTY;
and the land was filled with them."

◄ continue on page 74

שֶׁנֶּאֱמַר

אֲרַמִּי אֹבֵד אָבִי

וַיֵּרֶד מִצְרַיְמָה, וַיָּגָר שָׁם בִּמְתֵי מְעָט

וַיְהִי־שָׁם לְגוֹי גָּדוֹל עָצוּם וָרָב

וַיֵּרֶד מִצְרַיְמָה

אָנוּס עַל פִּי הַדִּבּוּר

וַיָּגָר שָׁם

מְלַמֵּד שֶׁלֹּא יָרַד יַעֲקֹב אָבִינוּ

לְהִשְׁתַּקֵּעַ בְּמִצְרַיִם, אֶלָּא לָגוּר שָׁם

שֶׁנֶּאֱמַר, וַיֹּאמְרוּ אֶל־פַּרְעֹה לָגוּר בָּאָרֶץ בָּאנוּ

כִּי־אֵין מִרְעֶה לַצֹּאן אֲשֶׁר לַעֲבָדֶיךָ

כִּי־כָבֵד הָרָעָב בְּאֶרֶץ כְּנָעַן

וְעַתָּה יֵשְׁבוּ־נָא עֲבָדֶיךָ בְּאֶרֶץ גֹּשֶׁן:

בִּמְתֵי מְעָט

כְּמָה שֶׁנֶּאֱמַר

בְּשִׁבְעִים נֶפֶשׁ יָרְדוּ אֲבֹתֶיךָ מִצְרָיְמָה

וְעַתָּה שָׂמְךָ יהוה אֱלֹהֶיךָ כְּכוֹכְבֵי הַשָּׁמַיִם לָרֹב:

וַיְהִי־שָׁם לְגוֹי

מְלַמֵּד שֶׁהָיוּ יִשְׂרָאֵל מְצֻיָּנִים שָׁם

גָּדוֹל עָצוּם

כְּמָה שֶׁנֶּאֱמַר

וּבְנֵי יִשְׂרָאֵל פָּרוּ וַיִּשְׁרְצוּ

וַיִּרְבּוּ וַיַּעַצְמוּ בִּמְאֹד מְאֹד

וַתִּמָּלֵא הָאָרֶץ אֹתָם:

◀ continue on page 74

When We Heard Your News
We Were Seized by a Great Joy

Amba Gualit, Sukkot 5669
(October 1908)

Blessed be the Lord God of Israel, the God of all spirits and flesh.

The present missive is being sent by the congregations of Israel in the communities of Abyssinia to our brethren in the congregations of Israel throughout the world.

Shalom, greetings to you, children of Israel, we hope that this letter finds you well.

The missive which you sent us with our teacher Yaakov Noah the son of Moshe Faitlovitch reached us and afforded us much pleasure.

Previously the fact of your existence was like a legend in our eyes, however we are now certain of the matter and very happy as a result. The news which we received from you strengthened our resolve and comforted our souls.

We are quite sad however. Please take pity on us and pray on our behalf.

With thanks to the Lord we still manage to this day to hold fast to our faith in a single God and the Torah of Moses. Until now, the Lord has not allowed the Seed of Jacob to be completely eradicated from the land of Abyssinia. In former times, we suffered great hardship and oppression, and many members of our community were forcibly converted to Christianity. Now, with thanks to the Lord, we have a kind king. Menelik wishes that every one of his subjects has the right to live according to the faith of his ancestors. May the Lord grant him long life. However, as we do not

have any schools and all of our sacred texts were destroyed, the missionaries have managed to mislead our brethren into betraying their faith by handing out the books of their false faith.

Now that we have heard your news we were seized by a great joy. The Jewish communities in Abyssinia are full of hope. Since our teacher Yaakov returned, all the Jews have turned their eyes and hopes towards you. Were we to receive books, schoolhouses and teachers so that our children would be able to learn, we would be greatly satisfied. Our own reserves are not sufficient to accomplish these tasks.

These days, we pray to the Lord that He should give long life to all the children of Israel, and to our teacher Yaakov in particular. Likewise, we pray that the Lord will enable us to meet our brethren face to face. May the Lord God of Abraham, Isaac, Jacob and Moses safeguard and watch over our teacher Yaakov Noah the son of Moshe.

The present letter was composed by the leaders and officials of the Jewish communities in the regions of Belesa, Wogera, Semien, Armacheo, Takusa and Dembiya, who came together for the Sukkot holiday to meet with our teacher Yaakov.

(Waldman, *From Ethiopia*, 98–99)

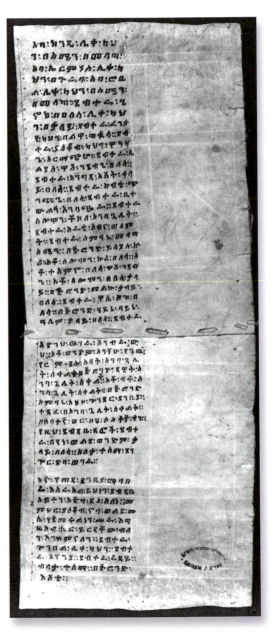

PRAYERS OF MOSES AGAINST PHARAOH

We shall tell you of all that was accomplished with the assistance of the present prayer, through which Moses was saved from the hand of Pharaoh.

The prayer of Moses. His supplication and plea, through which the Lord God caused his enemies to submit.

At first the angel Gabriel descended and spoke unto him saying: "Have no fear, Moses. Your prayer and plea were received by the Lord."

Moses rejoiced at the words of the angel and said: "Blessed be the Lord our God. From this point on I have no sadness in my soul."

Moses rose and made his way to Mount Sinai, as the angel of the Lord had commanded him to do. There, Moses prayed saying: "I sing of Your praise, O my Lord. May the glory of Your holy name be blessed. Please turn to me in my need. Awaken Your strength and go forth to secure our salvation. Save us and redeem us from the hand of Pharaoh."

After he had spoken these words, Pharaoh sent an emissary to Moses saying: "Shall you ascend to the heavens? There is no one who will save you from my hand. Therefore return to me. Behold I am coming to judge you in my anger and there is no one who will save you from my hand."

Moses replied saying: "Yet I have no fear of you. I will turn you into a reed with no strength, a leaf without wind. Behold the Lord will weaken your power and destroy you. He will cast you down from your throne and scatter you and your soldiers like dust. Whereas I shall be saved by the Lord from your hand."

When Pharaoh heard these words, he grew extremely angry. His heart burned within him like fire and he rubbed his head. He assembled all seventy-eight kings and there was only one man standing against them, named Moses. Other than Moses there was no other man standing there out of all the innumerable kings and officials.

And all the nations of the land and the kings and officers said to Pharaoh: "We have no other king but you, whatever you command us to do, we shall perform."

Then Pharaoh raised the image of a calf, made of gold and adorned with silver, and he said to them: "Bow down to this image of a calf." They all bowed down together as one and swore to murder Moses.

When the seventy-eight kings assembled and it became known to Moses that Pharaoh was

coming out against him, Moses fasted for forty days and nights and said: "Please hear my prayer and do not scorn my plea, for there is no other God but You, and I have no other Father or Master or Shepherd than you. You, O Lord, my God, shall be my Savior and Redeemer, for behold, Pharaoh is coming for me to wage war against me."

And the Lord heard his prayer and sent down sustenance for him, the savory manna, which

afforded great blessing and well-being, for it cannot be destroyed, and it never diminishes.

And the Lord spoke to Moses out of a column of clouds saying: "Have no fear, for I am the Lord your God."

When he saw the tongue of fire, Moses began to tremble and a great fear overtook him as he fell to the ground and became like a dead body. Then the Lord raised His voice saying: "Arise, my servant, my beloved. I am with you to strengthen you, and the entire universe shall be at your service. You shall see how I will scatter Pharaoh and his soldiers like dust in the sea."

When the Lord said these words to him, he began to sing praises and songs of Halleluya to the Lord.

And he wrote down the Lord's names…

Raise four stones from the waters and read out the prayer and wash yourself in the waters. Then cast the stones away. By this means your soul shall be redeemed and your oppressor shall succumb to you.

When you cast away the stones, your enemies shall flee and be seized by fear and tremble and scatter like dust, and their strength shall be as nothing more than a reed.

Take up the branches of an etrog tree in your right and left hands as you say the following: "Scatter all my enemies and haters like water and dust by the merit of these holy names of Yours.

By the merit of these holy names please bring me salvation. We shall be victorious and they shall be vanquished. When the sun rises, may the Lord rise and scatter your enemies and may all those who hate you flee before you. You are the Lord who has shown me compassion and provided me with these names. Holy, Holy, Holy."

And Moses stood outside the camp of the enemy… and, with a strike of the spear when Pharaoh banished him, continued: "Please scatter all my enemies and haters who seek to kill me. May they rather kill one another."

By the merit of these names of Yours, may our enemies and haters all be vanquished and may we be victorious. May their strength be cut down like a reed. Crush their bows and shatter their hands and legs. May each man weaken the other. May they weaken one another and be unable to harm us. Amen.

By the merit of these names of Yours, may they all flee before us, in every direction, and leave us in peace. Scatter them like dust in the depths of the sea. And the nation answered, Amen.

By the merit of these names of Yours, crush their shields and spears. May their arrows fall back upon their own heads and may they receive neither aid nor salvation.

By the merit of these names of Yours, annul their plans, darken their eyes and disrupt their inner thoughts. May their tongues deceive them and may all our enemies and haters be trampled like dust beneath our sandals. Amen.

By the merit of these names of Yours, overturn their homes and destroy their dwellings and the foundations of their houses. May the seed of their children be ruined and may all their deities be wiped out. May they be scattered like weeds in the fields.

By the merit of these names of Yours, annul their plans and scatter their assemblies. Seal their throats and still their tongues. Remove the bitterness of their poison. Do not allow anyone to speak who would rise up against me to curse me.

By the merit of these names of Yours, stop up their ears. May they be deaf and mute and completely unable to hear. May their eyelids grow weak and may their eyes be blinded so that they are unable to see.

By the merit of these names of Yours, pour out your anger upon them. Cast them away and uproot them forever and ever.

By the merit of these names of Yours, place fear in the hearts of my enemies and haters. Place them beneath the soles of my feet. May their flesh be left for the beasts in the fields and the birds of prey in the heavens, and may their blood flow like water.

By the merit of these names of Yours, lay waste to their lands and their possessions. Surround them and allow their enemies to chase them off.

O, my Lord, please do not grant them life and salvation, but rather land an almighty blow upon their heads. May they cut off and destroy one another and be unable to overtake us.

Crush their skulls and sever their necks and destroy them forever.

Exile them and cut them off from us. May they retreat as you bring down shame upon all my

enemies and haters who plotted to do me wrong and tried to kill me. May they be cursed and excommunicated in heaven as on earth. O, my Lord, cast down their souls. May they be like dry wood. Turn them into smoke, like a kernel of grain that has no life in it. Bring great hardship upon them. May their gold and silver be lost and may their clothing go up in flames. May their women and children be taken captive, may their cattle be taken off, and may we pursue them and overtake them.

O, my Lord, do not fulfill the requests of our enemies. Bring down disease and hardship upon them, raining down blows in Your anger. May they tremble before You. Confuse their thoughts. May all our haters flee before us and be shamed and cowed by our presence. Like water running over the earth, so shall their blood be spilled. Oppress them and uproot them. Drown at sea all our oppressors and haters who seek to kill us.

May their necks be severed with iron swords. May spears rain down upon them like water. Let a dense darkness descend upon them. May they be scattered and may their homes be destroyed.

O, my Lord, bind their hands and feet in shackles that shall never be undone and may we be victorious.

O, my Lord, pay them back in the same coin that they paid us, and increase their suffering. Destroy them and do not resurrect them forever and ever. Amen."

After Pharaoh had exiled Moses, he pursued him and caught up with him along the way. It was then that Moses offered up this prayer. He raised four stones in his hands, along with the dust of the earth, and he cast them among the enemies, saying: "Scatter these evildoers, these kings and officers of the land who have come to kill me. Show them your strength and authority,

my Lord, and place fear and awe in the hearts of my enemies and haters. O, my Lord, accept the prayers that rise from your faithful servants' lips and bring us salvation. Like a hen gathering her chicks beneath her wings, so shall You embrace us with Your right hand."

When Moses threw the four stones, he killed two hundred and forty-eight with the first stone, seven thousand and forty-two with the second stone, three thousand and eighty-eight with the third stone, and with the fourth stone…

When the Lord saw Moses warring with Pharaoh, he raised His voice to Moses saying: "Have no fear, for I am with you and shall save you. Rise now and head for the Red Sea. There you shall witness the great miracles that I shall perform on your behalf against Pharaoh."

Moses made his way with his soldiers who carried the Ark of the Covenant. And the angel Michael guided them during the day in a column of cloud and by night he guided them by the light of the fire.

When he arrived at the Red Sea with his soldiers, Moses rose and offered this prayer to the Lord. After he had entreated God's presence three times, he took up the branch of an etrog tree and smote the surface of the Red Sea saying: Rise up and fall silent on either side of us, at the behest of the Lord our God, until we shall have passed through to the other side. And the sea rose and stood in a column at either side. And the children of Israel passed through, carrying the Ark of the Covenant and singing songs in praise of the Lord.

In his pursuit of Moses, Pharaoh reached the Red Sea and entered with his entire army. And Pharaoh and all his soldiers drowned in the sea.

Then Moses said: May You be blessed, O Lord. For Your actions are wondrous and mighty

indeed. O Lord, You are rightfully deserving of praise in Zion.

And then they all spoke up as one, saying: "Let us sing to the Lord, for He is great and lofty, He cast down both horse and rider in the sea. He is my shield and succor, He is my salvation. This is my Lord and I shall exalt Him, He is my God, my Father, and I shall sing His praises. The Lord decides the battle, the Lord is His name. He sank Pharaoh's chariots and soldiers in the sea, and his most mighty riders and officers drowned in the deep. The waves have covered them forever."

Then the people began to dance, saying: "Who can compare to You, O holy One, awesome and praiseworthy, Worker of wonders."

After they had spoken these words while trampling the ground, the desert floor there never sprouted any grass ever again until this very day.

One hundred and forty kings were swept away, and the number of Moses' enemies who were taken off were eight hundred and twenty-six million, three hundred and fifty-nine thousand, five hundred and ninety-two.

(Arde'et, 54–64)

A Request to
Make Aliya

18th Adar I, 5695
(February 21, 1935)

DR. FAITLOVITCH'S SCHOOL
ADDIS-ABEBA. ABYSSINIA

ב"ה תרצ"ה לא אדר יח

הסתדרות הציונית
אל אדון רופין נ"ע

ומיושם.

א.נ.

הנני מודיע לכם כי הרבה כתבים באו אלי
...

Taamrat Emmanuel
Directeur de la „D: Faitlovitch School"
Addis Abeba
Abyssinie.

Dr. Faitlovitch, his sister Leah, Taamrat Emmanuel, the instructor, Reuven Isaiah, with students of the school, Addis Ababa, 1926

Dr. Faitlovitch, Taamrat Emmanuel, and students, Addis Ababa, 1931

AND POPULOUS

וָרָב

כְּמָה שֶׁנֶּאֱמַר

רְבָבָה כְּצֶמַח הַשָּׂדֶה נְתַתִּיךְ

וַתִּרְבִּי וַתִּגְדְּלִי, וַתָּבֹאִי בַּעֲדִי עֲדָיִים

שָׁדַיִם נָכֹנוּ וּשְׂעָרֵךְ צִמֵּחַ, וְאַתְּ עֵרֹם וְעֶרְיָה

וְיֵשׁ מוֹסִיפִים:

וָאֶעֱבֹר עָלַיִךְ וָאֶרְאֵךְ מִתְבּוֹסֶסֶת בְּדָמָיִךְ

וָאֹמַר לָךְ בְּדָמַיִךְ חֲיִי   וָאֹמַר לָךְ בְּדָמַיִךְ חֲיִי:

as it is said:

"I have CAUSED YOU TO MULTIPLY
like the plants of the field;
and you did increase and grow great,
and you did come to excellent beauty;
your breasts were formed,
and your hair was grown;
yet you were naked and bare."

Some add:
Now when I passed by you
and saw you wallowing in your blood,
I said to you: By your blood live;
and I said to you, By your blood live.

וַיָּרֵעוּ אֹתָנוּ הַמִּצְרִים וַיְעַנּוּנוּ

וַיִּתְּנוּ עָלֵינוּ עֲבֹדָה קָשָׁה:

AND THE EGYPTIANS DEALT ILL WITH US,

AND AFFLICTED US,

AND LAID UPON US HARD BONDAGE.

וַיָּרֵעוּ אֹתָנוּ הַמִּצְרִים

כְּמָה שֶׁנֶּאֱמַר

הָבָה נִּתְחַכְּמָה לוֹ

פֶּן־יִרְבֶּה

וְהָיָה כִּי־תִקְרֶאנָה מִלְחָמָה

וְנוֹסַף גַּם־הוּא עַל־שֹׂנְאֵינוּ

וְנִלְחַם־בָּנוּ, וְעָלָה מִן־הָאָרֶץ:

AND THE EGYPTIANS DEALT ILL WITH US

as it is said:
"Come, let us deal wisely with them,
lest they multiply,
and it come to pass,
that when any war should chance,
they too will join our enemies,
and fight against us,
and so go up out of the land."

וַיְעַנּוּנוּ

כְּמָה שֶׁנֶּאֱמַר

וַיָּשִׂימוּ עָלָיו שָׂרֵי מִסִּים

לְמַעַן עַנֹּתוֹ בְּסִבְלֹתָם

וַיִּבֶן עָרֵי מִסְכְּנוֹת לְפַרְעֹה

אֶת־פִּתֹם וְאֶת־רַעַמְסֵס:

AND AFFLICTED US

as it is said:
"Therefore
they did set over them taskmasters,
to AFFLICT them with their burdens.
And they built for Pharaoh treasure cities,
namely, Pitom and Ra'amses."

וַיִּתְּנוּ עָלֵינוּ עֲבֹדָה קָשָׁה

כְּמָה שֶׁנֶּאֱמַר

וַיַּעֲבִדוּ מִצְרַיִם אֶת־בְּנֵי יִשְׂרָאֵל בְּפָרֶךְ:

AND LAID UPON US HARD BONDAGE

as it is said:
"And Egypt made the children of Israel
serve with rigor."

74

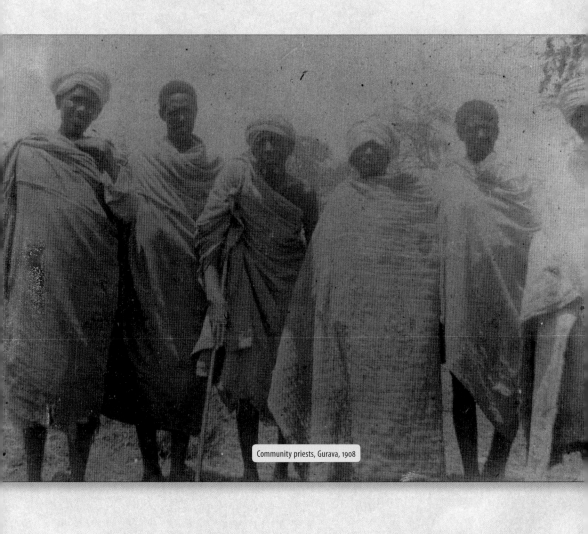

Community priests, Gurava, 1908

We Thought That with the Establishment of the State of Israel our Lot Would Also Improve

Yona Bogale, one of the leaders of Ethiopian Jewry, Addis Ababa, 1971

Yona Bogale, Addis Ababa,
23rd Cheshvan 5711 (November 3, 1950)

To my teacher and Rabbi, Dr. Yaakov Faitlovitch!

Since I cannot continue to remain silent I shall make an attempt to express my feelings and try to explain what is weighing heavily on my heart.

During your last visit to Addis Ababa, you advised me to make *aliya* to the land of Israel. At that time I was caught up in local national concerns…

With great shame and regret I now stand before you and look with fear upon the unfolding future. The children that the Lord granted me will be lost if I do not succeed in transferring them to the land of Israel. Just a year ago, I believed that the government of Israel would use its strength and influence to bring us to the Holy Land, and I thought that she would take up our cause as she has taken up the cause of so many other Jewish communities throughout the Diaspora. But to our great sorrow it appears that the State of Israel is not concerned with us. We are greatly afraid of what fate holds in store for us in the future. All the trials and tribulations which came upon the Jewish nation during its thousands of years of exile affected us as well because of our religion. We suffered the oppression typical of the Jewish nation. We thought that with the establishment of the State of Israel our lot would also improve. We thought that we too would make *aliya* along with the other communities of the nation in order to live a life of freedom in our own land. Shall we too have the great distinction of being among those who build up the state, or shall we be neglected and abandoned because of the particular color of our skin? Our excitement at the founding of the State of Israel was boundless. The complete

silence on the part of the authorities in Israel demonstrates that we are far from the hearts and minds of the nation. Perhaps I am mistaken?

Just a short while ago, a list of 200 family heads was compiled, consisting of the families who wish to make *aliya* with me to the land of Israel. Among the people listed are men who sold their cattle, abandoned their lands and made all the necessary preparations in order to make *aliya*: A number of young men from the Gondar region, which is two weeks' distance from here, came on foot to Addis Ababa. I was forced to inform them that the time has not yet come for us to make *aliya*. They returned, depressed and despondent, to the region of Gondar. All the Falashas desire to make *aliya* to the land of their forefathers, to work the land and defend it with their lives…

It is a full year that I have been meditating night and day on the idea of making *aliya* to Israel. If I were alone, I would travel on foot to Aden and from there to the land of our ancestors. But what do I do when I have a wife and children? How can I leave Abyssinia? I do not have the means to obtain a passport that would enable travel abroad. My great longing for the land of Israel gives me no rest. If you have an idea as to how to save me from these dire straits, I would be most grateful if you would write me…

(Collection, File 118)

וַנִּצְעַק אֶל־יְהוָה אֱלֹהֵי אֲבֹתֵינוּ
וַיִּשְׁמַע יְהוָה אֶת־קֹלֵנוּ
וַיַּרְא אֶת־עָנְיֵנוּ וְאֶת־עֲמָלֵנוּ
וְאֶת־לַחֲצֵנוּ:

AND WHEN WE CRIED
TO THE LORD GOD OF OUR FATHERS
THE LORD HEARD OUR VOICE,
AND LOOKED ON OUR AFFLICTION,
AND OUR TOIL, AND OUR OPPRESSIO

וַנִּצְעַק אֶל־יְהוָה אֱלֹהֵי אֲבֹתֵינוּ

**AND WHEN WE CRIED TO THE LORD
GOD OF OUR FATHERS**

כְּמָה שֶׁנֶּאֱמַר
וַיְהִי בַיָּמִים הָרַבִּים הָהֵם,
וַיָּמָת מֶלֶךְ מִצְרַיִם
וַיֵּאָנְחוּ בְנֵי־יִשְׂרָאֵל מִן־הָעֲבֹדָה,
וַיִּזְעָקוּ
וַתַּעַל שַׁוְעָתָם אֶל־הָאֱלֹהִים מִן־הָעֲבֹדָה:

as it is said:
"And it came to pass
in the course of those many days,
that the king of Egypt died,
and the children of Israel
sighed by reason of the bondage,
and they CRIED out;
and their cry came up to God
by reason of the bondage."

וַיִּשְׁמַע יְהוָה אֶת־קֹלֵנוּ

THE LORD HEARD OUR VOICE

כְּמָה שֶׁנֶּאֱמַר
וַיִּשְׁמַע אֱלֹהִים אֶת־נַאֲקָתָם
וַיִּזְכֹּר אֱלֹהִים אֶת־בְּרִיתוֹ
אֶת־אַבְרָהָם אֶת־יִצְחָק וְאֶת־יַעֲקֹב:

as it is said:
"And God HEARD their groaning,
and God remembered His covenant
with Abraham, with Isaac, and with Jacob

וַיַּרְא אֶת־עָנְיֵנוּ

AND LOOKED ON OUR AFFLICTION

זוֹ פְּרִישׁוּת דֶּרֶךְ אֶרֶץ
כְּמָה שֶׁנֶּאֱמַר
וַיַּרְא אֱלֹהִים אֶת־בְּנֵי יִשְׂרָאֵל
וַיֵּדַע אֱלֹהִים:

this refers
to their separation from their wives,
as it is said:
"And God saw the children of Israel,
and God knew."

◂ continue on page 81

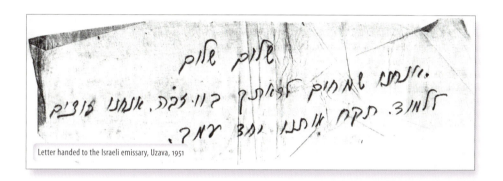

Letter handed to the Israeli emissary, Uzava, 1951

The Jewish school in Teda, 1976

The first youth group before heading off to school in Kfar Batya, Israel, Addis Ababa, 1955

Students of the Jewish Agency seminar, Asmara, 1956

JUST AS GOD REDEEMED MOSES

[…] Just as God redeemed Moses from the hand of King Pharaoh […] And Moses fled before Pharaoh and settled in Meri [?] and Midian – so shall you redeem me now, my Lord and the Lord of my forefathers. Hear my plea, O my Master, hear my prayer. Redeem Your faithful servant from all his troubles and hardships.

Just as God redeemed Israel from the hand of King Pharaoh, them and their fathers, after two hundred and forty years of slavery in the land of Egypt, and the Lord heard their cries and beheld their suffering, the Lord saw the children of Israel and redeemed them on that very day – so shall You redeem me, my Lord and the Lord of my forefathers. Hear my prayer, O my Master, hear my plea. Redeem your faithful servant from all his troubles and hardships.

(Eshkoli, 132)

Community priests in the synagogue in Ambover, 1976

וְאֶת־עֲמָלֵנוּ

אֵלּוּ הַבָּנִים

כְּמָה שֶׁנֶּאֱמַר

כָּל־הַבֵּן הַיִּלּוֹד, הַיְאֹרָה תַּשְׁלִיכֻהוּ

וְכָל־הַבַּת תְּחַיּוּן:

AND OUR TOIL
> this refers to the sons,
> as it is said:
> "every son that is born
> you shall cast into the River,
> and every daughter
> you shall save alive."

וְאֶת־לַחֲצֵנוּ

זֶה הַדְּחַק

כְּמָה שֶׁנֶּאֱמַר

וְגַם־רָאִיתִי אֶת־הַלַּחַץ

אֲשֶׁר מִצְרַיִם לֹחֲצִים אֹתָם:

AND OUR OPPRESSION
> this refers to the force used,
> as it is said:
> "And I have also seen
> the OPPRESSION
> with which Egypt oppresses them."

**AND THE LORD BROUGHT US OUT OF EGYPT
WITH A MIGHTY HAND,
AND WITH AN OUTSTRETCHED ARM,
AND WITH GREAT TERROR, AND WITH SIGNS
AND WITH WONDERS.**

AND THE LORD BROUGHT US OUT OF EGYPT
    not by an angel,
    nor by a Seraph,
    nor by a messenger,
    but the Holy One, blessed is He, He Himself,
    in His glory,

    as it is said:
  "For I will pass through the land of Egypt this night,
   and I will smite all the firstborn in the land of Egypt,
   both man and beast, and against all the gods of Egypt
   I will execute judgments; I am the LORD."

For I will pass through the land of Egypt	I Myself, not an angel:
And I will smite all the firstborn	I Myself, not a Seraph:
And against all the gods of Egypt	
I will execute judgments	I Myself, not a messenger;
I am the LORD	I am He, no other.

Community priest, 1937

WITH A MIGHTY HAND
    this refers to the cattle plague,
    as it is said:
  "Behold, the HAND of the LORD
   will be on your cattle in the field,
   upon the horses,
   upon the asses,
   upon the camels,
   upon the oxen,
   and upon the sheep:
   there shall be a very grievous plague."

וַיּוֹצִאֵנוּ יהוה מִמִּצְרַיִם
בְּיָד חֲזָקָה וּבִזְרֹעַ נְטוּיָה, וּבְמֹרָא גָּדֹל
וּבְאֹתוֹת וּבְמֹפְתִים:

וַיּוֹצִאֵנוּ יהוה מִמִּצְרַיִם

לֹא עַל יְדֵי מַלְאָךְ
וְלֹא עַל יְדֵי שָׂרָף
וְלֹא עַל יְדֵי שָׁלֵיחַ
אֶלָּא הַקָּדוֹשׁ בָּרוּךְ הוּא בִּכְבוֹדוֹ וּבְעַצְמוֹ

שֶׁנֶּאֱמַר
וְעָבַרְתִּי בְאֶרֶץ־מִצְרַיִם בַּלַּיְלָה הַזֶּה
וְהִכֵּיתִי כָל־בְּכוֹר בְּאֶרֶץ מִצְרַיִם, מֵאָדָם וְעַד־בְּהֵמָה
וּבְכָל־אֱלֹהֵי מִצְרַיִם אֶעֱשֶׂה שְׁפָטִים
אֲנִי יהוה:

אֲנִי וְלֹא מַלְאָךְ	וְעָבַרְתִּי בְאֶרֶץ־מִצְרַיִם
אֲנִי וְלֹא שָׂרָף	וְהִכֵּיתִי כָל־בְּכוֹר
אֲנִי וְלֹא הַשָּׁלֵיחַ	וּבְכָל־אֱלֹהֵי מִצְרַיִם אֶעֱשֶׂה שְׁפָטִים
אֲנִי הוּא וְלֹא אַחֵר	אֲנִי יהוה

בְּיָד חֲזָקָה
זוֹ הַדֶּבֶר
כְּמָה שֶׁנֶּאֱמַר
הִנֵּה יַד־יהוה הוֹיָה בְּמִקְנְךָ אֲשֶׁר בַּשָּׂדֶה
בַּסּוּסִים בַּחֲמֹרִים בַּגְּמַלִּים, בַּבָּקָר וּבַצֹּאן
דֶּבֶר כָּבֵד מְאֹד:

AND WITH AN OUTSTRETCHED ARM
    that refers to the sword,
    as it is said:
   "And a drawn sword in His hand
   STRETCHED OUT over Jerusalem."

AND WITH GREAT TERROR
    this refers to the feelings of the people
    when God revealed before their eyes
    the glory of His Presence,
    as it is said:
   "Or has God ventured to go and take Him a nation
    from the midst of another nation,
    by trials, by signs, and by wonders, and by wars,
    and by a mighty hand, and by an outstretched arm,
    and by great terrors,
    according to all that the LORD your God
    did for you in Egypt,
    before your eyes?"

AND WITH SIGNS
    this refers to the rod,
    as it is said:
   "And you shall take in your hands this rod,
    with which you shall do the SIGNS."

AND WITH WONDERS
    this refers to the blood.
    as it is said:
   "And I will show WONDERS
    in the heavens and on the earth:

וּבִזְרֹעַ נְטוּיָה

זוֹ הַחֶרֶב
כְּמָה שֶׁנֶּאֱמַר
וְחַרְבּוֹ שְׁלוּפָה בְּיָדוֹ
נְטוּיָה עַל־יְרוּשָׁלָ͏ִם:

וּבְמֹרָא גָּדֹל

זֶה גִּלּוּי שְׁכִינָה
כְּמָה שֶׁנֶּאֱמַר
אוֹ הֲנִסָּה אֱלֹהִים לָבוֹא לָקַחַת לוֹ גוֹי מִקֶּרֶב גּוֹי
בְּמַסֹּת בְּאֹתֹת וּבְמוֹפְתִים וּבְמִלְחָמָה
וּבְיָד חֲזָקָה, וּבִזְרוֹעַ נְטוּיָה
וּבְמוֹרָאִים גְּדֹלִים
כְּכֹל אֲשֶׁר־עָשָׂה לָכֶם יְהוָה אֱלֹהֵיכֶם בְּמִצְרַיִם
לְעֵינֶיךָ:

וּבְאֹתוֹת

זֶה הַמַּטֶּה
כְּמָה שֶׁנֶּאֱמַר
וְאֶת־הַמַּטֶּה הַזֶּה תִּקַּח בְּיָדֶךָ
אֲשֶׁר תַּעֲשֶׂה־בּוֹ אֶת־הָאֹתֹת:

וּבְמֹפְתִים

זֶה הַדָּם
כְּמָה שֶׁנֶּאֱמַר
וְנָתַתִּי מוֹפְתִים בַּשָּׁמַיִם וּבָאָרֶץ

Community priest, 1937

It is customary to spill a drop of wine from the cup as each wonder is mentioned:

BLOOD, AND FIRE, AND PILLARS OF SMOKE."

Another explanation is as follows:

"mighty hand" *(two words)*		two plagues:
"outstretched arm" *(two words)*		another two:
"great terror" *(two words)*		another two:
"signs" *(the plural)*		another two:
"wonders" *(the plural)*		another two:

THAT MAKES UP THE TEN PLAGUES

which the Holy One, blessed is He, brought

on the Egyptians in Egypt.

And here they are:

It is customary to spill a drop of wine from the cup as each plague, and each of the acronyms, Dezakh, Adash and Be'aḥav, is mentioned:

BLOOD	FROGS	LICE
BEASTS	CATTLE-PLAGUE	BOILS
HAIL	LOCUSTS	DARKNESS

SLAYING OF THE FIRSTBORN

Rabbi Yehuda used to abbreviate them as follows:

DEZAKH ADASH BE'AḤAV

נוהגים להטיף מעט יין מן הכוס על כל מופת שמזכירים:

דָּם וָאֵשׁ וְתִימְרוֹת עָשָׁן:

דָּבָר אַחֵר

שְׁתַּיִם	בְּיָד חֲזָקָה
שְׁתַּיִם	וּבִזְרֹעַ נְטוּיָה
שְׁתַּיִם	וּבְמֹרָא גָּדֹל
שְׁתַּיִם	וּבְאֹתוֹת
שְׁתַּיִם	וּבְמֹפְתִים

אֵלּוּ עֶשֶׂר מַכּוֹת

שֶׁהֵבִיא הַקָּדוֹשׁ בָּרוּךְ הוּא
עַל הַמִּצְרִים בְּמִצְרַיִם
וְאֵלּוּ הֵן

נוהגים להטיף מעט יין מן הכוס כשמזכירים כל מכה ומכה
ועל "דצ"ך עד"ש באח"ב" ואומרים:

כִּנִּים	צְפַרְדֵּעַ	דָּם
שְׁחִין	דֶּבֶר	עָרוֹב
חֹשֶׁךְ	אַרְבֶּה	בָּרָד

מַכַּת בְּכוֹרוֹת.

רַבִּי יְהוּדָה הָיָה נוֹתֵן בָּהֶם סִימָנִים
דְּצַ"ךְ עַדַ"שׁ בְּאַחַ"ב

87

רַ**בִּי** יוֹסֵי הַגְּלִילִי אוֹמֵר

מִנַּיִן אַתָּה אוֹמֵר
שֶׁלָּקוּ הַמִּצְרִים בְּמִצְרַיִם עֶשֶׂר מַכּוֹת
וְעַל הַיָּם לָקוּ חֲמִשִּׁים מַכּוֹת

בְּמִצְרַיִם
מַה הוּא אוֹמֵר
וַיֹּאמְרוּ הַחַרְטֻמִּם אֶל־פַּרְעֹה
אֶצְבַּע אֱלֹהִים הִוא:

וְעַל הַיָּם
מַה הוּא אוֹמֵר
וַיַּרְא יִשְׂרָאֵל אֶת־הַיָּד הַגְּדֹלָה
אֲשֶׁר עָשָׂה יְהוָה בְּמִצְרַיִם
וַיִּירְאוּ הָעָם אֶת־יְהוָה
וַיַּאֲמִינוּ בַּיהוָה וּבְמֹשֶׁה עַבְדּוֹ:

RABBI

Yose the Galilean asked,
How can we tell
that the Egyptians who were punished
with ten plagues in Egypt,
were afterwards punished
with fifty at the sea?

In Egypt what expression was used?
"Then the magicians said to Pharaoh,
That is the FINGER of God."

At the sea what expression was used?
"And Israel saw the great HAND
which the LORD laid on Egypt:
and the people feared the LORD,
and they believed in the LORD
and in His servant Moses."

Community priest, 1937

88

Bringing the Beta Israel in Abyssinia Closer to Klal Yisrael

Kes Uri Ben Baruch

Asmara, 25th Elul 5714
(September 23, 1954)

To our master, the great, accomplished Rabbi, lover of Beta Israel
Rabbi Ze'ev Gold, may he be granted long life
Member of the Directorate of the Jewish Agency and Head of the Department of Jewish Culture, The Holy City of Jerusalem

May you be sealed in the Book of Life.

It is with great joy that we write to inform the esteemed Rabbi, the father figure so concerned with the welfare of the Beta Israel in Abyssinia, that on the Thursday of the Torah portion *Nitzavim* in the year 5714, with the Lord's help, the first Jewish school for the Ethiopian Jewish community will open for religious and Hebrew-language studies in the town of Uzava. This is the most momentous event in the history of the Falashas. We see the events of these days as a matter full of great symbolism, like the events transcribed by Ezra the scribe in his day. We have also just witnessed the publication of the first pamphlet in Amharic concerning the Jewish holidays.

It is with great emotion, reverence and much love that we would like to express our heartfelt thanks for the great effort undertaken on our behalf by the esteemed Rabbi, as he took care to see to all these details via his faithful emissary, Rabbi Samuel Be'eri, who has been working diligently on our behalf, providing education and guidance and bringing the Beta Israel in Abyssinia closer to *Klal Yisrael*. Our sages, may they rest in peace, said: "Anyone who saves the life of a single member of the Jewish community is considered to have saved an entire world." How great then is the gift of our teacher and Rabbi who has saved tens of thousands of Jewish souls through his sacred works. Words cannot suffice to express our gratitude.

Our prayers, and the prayers of the entire Beta Israel in Abyssinia, are that this New Year, which is now upon us, should be a bountiful year. May the good Lord grant the esteemed Rabbi long life and may he merit to see the ingathering of exiles in his days. May he be written into the Book of Life alongside the righteous for a life of goodness and peace, and may he merit to raise generations of fine children, who observe the Torah and perform good deeds. May the Lord grant him years of plenty, health, and happiness. May we merit witnessing the final redemption this year with the arrival of the Messiah. Amen.

Respectfully yours,
The Heads of the Jewish Community
of the Beta Israel in Abyssinia:
Uri ben Baruch
Abraham ben Simcha
Berachyahu ben Yalin
Raphael ben Tekuye
Sasson Asher
Yona Bogale

(*Aliya* department)

כַּמָּה לָקוּ בְאֶצְבַּע
עֶשֶׂר מַכּוֹת.
אֱמֹר מֵעַתָּה
בְּמִצְרַיִם לָקוּ עֶשֶׂר מַכּוֹת
וְעַל הַיָּם לָקוּ חֲמִשִּׁים מַכּוֹת.

Now what punishment
did they receive from the finger?
Ten plagues.
Deduce from this that
if they had TEN plagues from the FINGER,
then at the sea, where it says HAND,
they must have had FIFTY plagues.

Rabbi Eliezer asked, How can we tell that every single plague
which the Holy One, blessed is He,
inflicted on the Egyptians in Egypt,
was in reality FOUR plagues?
We know this from the verse:
"He cast upon them His fierce anger:
wrath, and indignation, and trouble,
an embassy of evil messengers."

"Wrath"	makes	one
"indignation"	makes	two
"trouble"	makes	three
"an embassy of evil messengers"	makes	four.

Deduce from this
THAT IN EGYPT (WITH THE FINGER)
THEY MUST HAVE HAD IN REALITY FORTY PLAGUES,
AND AT THE SEA (WITH THE HAND)
THEY MUST HAVE HAD TWO HUNDRED PLAGUES.

רַבִּי אֱלִיעֶזֶר אוֹמֵר מִנַּיִן שֶׁכָּל מַכָּה וּמַכָּה
שֶׁהֵבִיא הַקָּדוֹשׁ בָּרוּךְ הוּא עַל הַמִּצְרִים בְּמִצְרַיִם
הָיְתָה שֶׁל אַרְבַּע מַכּוֹת
שֶׁנֶּאֱמַר: יְשַׁלַּח־בָּם חֲרוֹן אַפּוֹ
עֶבְרָה וָזַעַם וְצָרָה, מִשְׁלַחַת מַלְאֲכֵי רָעִים:

אַחַת	עֶבְרָה
שְׁתַּיִם	וָזַעַם
שָׁלוֹשׁ	וְצָרָה
אַרְבַּע	מִשְׁלַחַת מַלְאֲכֵי רָעִים

אֱמֹר מֵעַתָּה

בְּמִצְרַיִם לָקוּ אַרְבָּעִים מַכּוֹת

וְעַל הַיָּם לָקוּ מָאתַיִם מַכּוֹת.

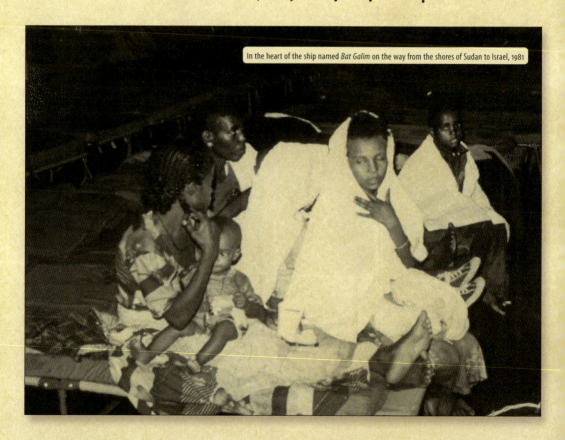

In the heart of the ship named *Bat Galim* on the way from the shores of Sudan to Israel, 1981

Rabbi Akiva asked, How can we tell that every single plague
    which the Holy One, blessed is He,
    inflicted on the Egyptians in Egypt,
    was in reality FIVE plagues?
    We know this from the verse:
    "He cast upon them
    His fierce anger, wrath, and indignation, and trouble,
    an embassy of evil messengers."

"Fierce anger"	makes	one
"wrath"	makes	two
"indignation"	makes	three
"trouble"	makes	four
"an embassy of evil messengers"	makes	five.

    Deduce from this

THAT IN EGYPT (WITH THE FINGER)
    THEY MUST HAVE HAD FIFTY PLAGUES,

AND AT THE SEA (WITH THE HAND)
    THEY MUST HAVE HAD TWO HUNDRED AND FIFTY PLAGUES.

רַבִּי עֲקִיבָא אוֹמֵר מִנַּיִן שֶׁכָּל מַכָּה וּמַכָּה

שֶׁהֵבִיא הַקָּדוֹשׁ בָּרוּךְ הוּא עַל הַמִּצְרִים בְּמִצְרַיִם

הָיְתָה שֶׁל חָמֵשׁ מַכּוֹת

שֶׁנֶּאֱמַר: יְשַׁלַּח־בָּם

חֲרוֹן אַפּוֹ, עֶבְרָה וָזַעַם וְצָרָה, מִשְׁלַחַת מַלְאֲכֵי רָעִים:

חֲרוֹן אַפּוֹ	אַחַת
עֶבְרָה	שְׁתַּיִם
וָזַעַם	שָׁלוֹשׁ
וְצָרָה	אַרְבַּע
מִשְׁלַחַת מַלְאֲכֵי רָעִים	חָמֵשׁ

אֱמֹר מֵעַתָּה

בְּמִצְרַיִם לָקוּ חֲמִשִּׁים מַכּוֹת

וְעַל הַיָּם לָקוּ חֲמִשִּׁים וּמָאתַיִם מַכּוֹת.

ב"ה כ"א באייר תשל"א 16-5-1971

אנו היהודים שנמצאים באתיופיה הנה עברו ארבע שנים ושבעה חודשים מאז שהקמנו חברה חדשה. שנקראת בשם חברת היהודים שלום באתיופיה. מטרת החברה להפיץ את חק התורה ואת דת היהודי ולהציל את היהודים ששכחו את אלהים את התורה ואת שבטם. שמספרם מגיע לחמשים אלף ולמעלה שנמצאים בהררי חבש. שחייהם הם בחיי החושך. בלחץ וברדיפות הגויים. ולהקים קשר בין היהודים (הפלאשים) שנמצאים ובין היהודים שבציון. הרבה גויים התייעצו ואמרו באו נשמיד את היהודים ונמחה את שמם. תהילים פרק 83 פסוק 4. הנה הרבה מסיונרים שנשלחו מהגויים דורשים לנו הרבה צרות בלי סוף. בעצת הגויים וברדיפות המסיונרים מספר גדול של פלאשים נמצאים כלואים בחיי החושך. הנה רוצים לכלותינו את הפלאשים שנשארו לאות. שיר השירים פרקים 5.4.2 ואמרו בשועלים השמידו את הכרם וקמנו לגרש את השועלים והכרם הוא בית ישראל. תהילים פרק 80 פסוק 8-15 את היוצא ממצרים תטע החצרים כדי שהחצרים לשועלים שלא ישמידו את הכרם נצור חכמי ישראל לשמור את זה. יחזקאל פרק 34 פסוק 16 ויאמר אלה בעת שנמצאה אשיב את — הנדחה אחבש את הנשברה וארפא את החולה.

אשלח את הציידים לצוד אותכם במדבר והמדבר הוא בית הרעם והציידים הם מנהיגי ישראל בוא נוציא את אלה שנמצאים במדבר שעזבו את התורה ששכחו את ירושלים. ירמיהו פרק 16 פסוק 16. מטרת החברה שלנו לשמור את היהודים שלא יעזבו את דתם ולחבש את היהודים שבציון. בקרב הגויים בתפוצות ארץ חבש. לבנות בית ספר בכל מקום אשר שם נמצאים הפלאשים ולהקים בית כנסת שילמדו בהם עברית ולהפיץ את חיי הישראלים ואת מנהגיהם. נבקשכם שתושיטו את עזרתכם למען השבט הנדח הזה. תכירו את חברתנו ותקשרו את רבני ישראל עם רבני הפלאשים שנגדל אותו ונעבדו.

בכבוד רב.

מראשי החברה.

א. הכהן אורי בן ברוך נשיא החברה
ב. זולה תשמה סלן נשיא החברה
ג. נגוסה יעקב יוסף
ד. הכהן שמחה נגת יוסף
ה. אהרון ברוק. מאזין החברה
ו. תשלה מקונן סלן מזכירה של החברה
ז. אברהם אשכול מזכירה של החברה
ח. עקיבא אורי מזכיר החברה
ט. יאיר אורי (אברהם ברהן) אחראי של החברה.

Bringing Back the Jews that Disappeared

Wolleka, 21st Iyar 5731 (May 16, 1971)

For the members of the Jewish community residing in Ethiopia it has been four years and seven months now since we founded a new cooperative known as the Cooperative of Jews Living in Ethiopia. The purpose of the cooperative is to spread the laws of the Torah and the Jewish religion and to bring back the Jews who have forgotten their homeland, the Torah, and their tribe, who number upwards of 50,000, scattered throughout the hills of Abyssinia, who live their lives in darkness, oppressed and harassed by the non-Jews, in the hopes of establishing a bridge between the remaining Jews (Falashas) and those who disappeared.

Many non-Jews have conspired, saying: Let us destroy the Jews and erase their name" (in accordance with Psalms 83:5). Indeed, there are many missionaries who have been sent to us by the non-Jews who cause us endless troubles. As a result of the conspiracies of the non-Jews and the pursuit of the missionaries, a great number of Falashas have been swallowed up by lives of darkness. They are on the verge of wiping us out, we Falashas who have persevered as a sign and a symbol.

In the book of Jeremiah 16:16, it is written: I shall send forth the hunters and they shall hunt you from the cave – the cave is the house of the nation and the hunters are the leaders of Israel. Come let us bring forth those who are stuck in the cave, those who have abandoned the Torah and forgotten Jerusalem. The activities of our cooperative include making sure that Jews do not abandon their faith and to seek out Jews who disappeared into the midst of the non-Jewish population throughout the lands of Abyssinia. We also intend to found a school in any location where Falashas have been scattered, along with a synagogue where all will be able to learn Hebrew and develop Jewish lives replete with the appropriate customs. We are writing to ask you to extend your assistance to this neglected tribe. Get to know our cooperative and establish connections between the Rabbis of Israel and the Rabbis among the Falashas so that we might receive vital advice and support.

Respectfully yours,
The Heads of the Cooperative,
Uri ben Baruch, Kohen
President of the Cooperative
[Eight additional signatures appear – Ed.]

(M.W.A.)

HOW MANY GOOD THINGS
HAS THE ALMIGHTY SHOWERED ON US!

IF He had brought us out of Egypt,
   BUT without bringing judgments on our enemies   **GOOD ENOUGH**

IF He had brought judgments down on them,
   BUT without judging their idols   **GOOD ENOUGH**

IF He had judged their idols,
   BUT without slaying their firstborn   **GOOD ENOUGH**

IF He had slain their firstborn,
   BUT without giving us their wealth   **GOOD ENOUGH**

IF He had given us their wealth,
   BUT without dividing the sea for us   **GOOD ENOUGH**

IF He had divided the sea for us,
   BUT without leading us across on dry land   **GOOD ENOUGH**

IF He had led us across on dry land,
   BUT without sinking our enemies in its depths   **GOOD ENOUGH**

IF He had sunk our enemies in its depths,
   BUT without supplying our needs in the desert,*   **GOOD ENOUGH**

IF He had supplied our needs in the desert,*
   BUT without feeding us with manna   **GOOD ENOUGH**

IF He had fed us with manna,
   BUT without granting us the Sabbath   **GOOD ENOUGH**

IF He had granted us the Sabbath,
   BUT without bringing us to Mount Sinai   **GOOD ENOUGH**

IF He had brought us to Mount Sinai,
   BUT without giving us the Torah   **GOOD ENOUGH**

IF He had given us the Torah,
   BUT without bringing us into the land of Israel   **GOOD ENOUGH**

IF He had brought us into the land of Israel,
   BUT without building us the Temple   **GOOD ENOUGH**

* for forty years

כַּמָּה מַעֲלוֹת טוֹבוֹת לַמָּקוֹם עָלֵינוּ

		דַּיֵּנוּ
אִלּוּ הוֹצִיאָנוּ מִמִּצְרַיִם	וְלֹא עָשָׂה בָהֶם שְׁפָטִים	דַּיֵּנוּ
אִלּוּ עָשָׂה בָהֶם שְׁפָטִים	וְלֹא עָשָׂה בֵאלֹהֵיהֶם	דַּיֵּנוּ
אִלּוּ עָשָׂה בֵאלֹהֵיהֶם	וְלֹא הָרַג אֶת בְּכוֹרֵיהֶם	דַּיֵּנוּ
אִלּוּ הָרַג אֶת בְּכוֹרֵיהֶם	וְלֹא נָתַן לָנוּ אֶת מָמוֹנָם	דַּיֵּנוּ
אִלּוּ נָתַן לָנוּ אֶת מָמוֹנָם	וְלֹא קָרַע לָנוּ אֶת הַיָּם	דַּיֵּנוּ
אִלּוּ קָרַע לָנוּ אֶת הַיָּם	וְלֹא הֶעֱבִירָנוּ בְתוֹכוֹ בֶּחָרָבָה	דַּיֵּנוּ
אִלּוּ הֶעֱבִירָנוּ בְתוֹכוֹ בֶּחָרָבָה	וְלֹא שִׁקַּע צָרֵינוּ בְּתוֹכוֹ	דַּיֵּנוּ
אִלּוּ שִׁקַּע צָרֵינוּ בְּתוֹכוֹ	וְלֹא סִפֵּק צָרְכֵּנוּ בַּמִּדְבָּר*	דַּיֵּנוּ
אִלּוּ סִפֵּק צָרְכֵּנוּ בַּמִּדְבָּר*	וְלֹא הֶאֱכִילָנוּ אֶת הַמָּן	דַּיֵּנוּ
אִלּוּ הֶאֱכִילָנוּ אֶת הַמָּן	וְלֹא נָתַן לָנוּ אֶת הַשַּׁבָּת	דַּיֵּנוּ
אִלּוּ נָתַן לָנוּ אֶת הַשַּׁבָּת	וְלֹא קֵרְבָנוּ לִפְנֵי הַר סִינַי	דַּיֵּנוּ
אִלּוּ קֵרְבָנוּ לִפְנֵי הַר סִינַי	וְלֹא נָתַן לָנוּ אֶת הַתּוֹרָה	דַּיֵּנוּ
אִלּוּ נָתַן לָנוּ אֶת הַתּוֹרָה	וְלֹא הִכְנִיסָנוּ לְאֶרֶץ יִשְׂרָאֵל	דַּיֵּנוּ
אִלּוּ הִכְנִיסָנוּ לְאֶרֶץ יִשְׂרָאֵל	וְלֹא בָנָה לָנוּ אֶת בֵּית הַבְּחִירָה	דַּיֵּנוּ

* אַרְבָּעִים שָׁנָה

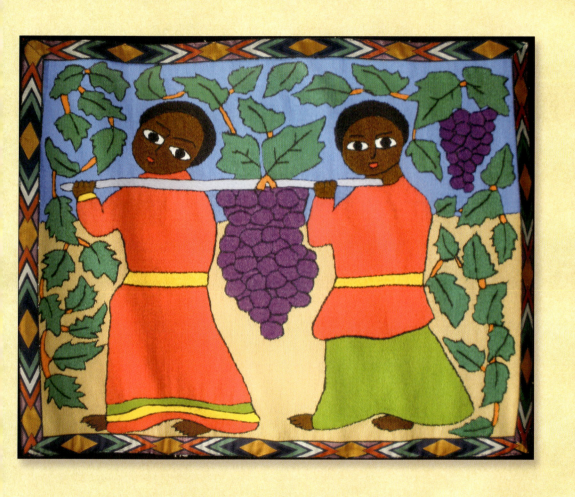

עַל אַחַת כַּמָּה וְכַמָּה
טוֹבָה כְּפוּלָה וּמְכֻפֶּלֶת לַמָּקוֹם עָלֵינוּ

וְעָשָׂה בָהֶם שְׁפָטִים	שֶׁהוֹצִיאָנוּ מִמִּצְרַיִם
וְהָרַג בְּכוֹרֵיהֶם	וְעָשָׂה בֵאלֹהֵיהֶם
וְקָרַע לָנוּ אֶת הַיָּם	וְנָתַן לָנוּ אֶת מָמוֹנָם
וְשִׁקַּע צָרֵינוּ בְּתוֹכוֹ	וְהֶעֱבִירָנוּ בְּתוֹכוֹ בֶּחָרָבָה
וְהֶאֱכִילָנוּ אֶת הַמָּן	וְסִפֵּק צָרְכֵּנוּ בַּמִּדְבָּר אַרְבָּעִים שָׁנָה
וְקֵרְבָנוּ לִפְנֵי הַר סִינַי	וְנָתַן לָנוּ אֶת הַשַּׁבָּת
וְהִכְנִיסָנוּ לְאֶרֶץ יִשְׂרָאֵל	וְנָתַן לָנוּ אֶת הַתּוֹרָה
לְכַפֵּר עַל כָּל עֲוֹנוֹתֵינוּ.	וּבָנָה לָנוּ אֶת בֵּית הַבְּחִירָה

**HOW MUCH GREATER THEN, INCALCULABLY GREAT,
ARE THE BENEFITS WHICH GOD DID SHOWER UPON US
IN DOUBLE AND REDOUBLED MEASURE!**

For He DID bring us out of Egypt;
He DID bring judgments down on our enemies;

He DID judge their idols;
He DID slay their firstborn;

He DID give us their wealth;
He DID divide the sea for us;

He DID lead us across on dry land;
He DID sink our enemies in its depths;

He DID supply our needs in the desert for forty years;
He DID feed us with manna;

He DID give us the Sabbath;
He DID bring us to Mount Sinai;

He DID give us the Torah;
He DID bring us to the land of Israel;

He DID build us the Temple,
TO ATONE FOR ALL OUR SINS.

◀ continue on page 104

Community priest, 1937

Those You Redeemed with your Might

A PRAYER FOR THE PASSOVER HOLIDAY

Those You redeemed with your might,
Leading them out of the land of Egypt.

Those You redeemed with your might,
Leading them out of the impure land.

Those You redeemed with your might,
Rescuing them from the army of Pharaoh.

Those You redeemed with your might,
Guiding them with Your holy cloud.

Those You redeemed with your might,
Leading them at night in a column of fire.

Those You redeemed with your might,
Guiding them for forty years through the desert.

Those You redeemed with your might,
Sending down manna for them from heaven.

Those You redeemed with your might,
Feeding them the manna in the desert.

Those You redeemed with your might,
As they were sustained by the manna for forty years.

Those You redeemed with your might,
Bequeathing Your people to Joshua and Caleb.

Those You redeemed with your might,
Bringing them to the border of Penuel.

Those You redeemed with your might,
Taking them as Yours and planting them firmly.

Those You redeemed with your might,
Settling them down in the place You had prepared.

Those You redeemed with your might,
That they might bring forth milk and honey.

Those You redeemed with your might,
That the grains and vines might flourish.

Blessed are You, O Lord, Who gave us the Holy Sabbath.
Blessed are You, O Lord, Who gave us the Ten Commandments.
Blessed are You, O Lord, Who gave us honored holidays and festivals.

You have brought loving-kindness and compassion upon us;
That we might stand before Your countenance…

(Ben Dor, 19–20)

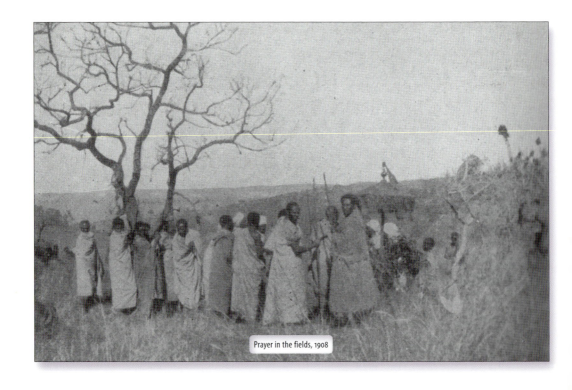

Prayer in the fields, 1908

להוד כ.לתו

מר יצחק רבין

ראש ממשלת ישראל

ירושלים, ישראל

כבוד ראש הממשלה,

כדברי הנביא "מה נאוו על ההרים רגלי מבשר מבשר שלום מבשר טוב משמיע ישועה' בשבועות שעברו אנו יהודי אתיופיה הפלסים התבשרנו בהודעה שנמסרה ע"י צוות בינ- מסרדי המקבלת החליטה לכלול את יהודי אתיופיה הפלסים בתוך כלל ישראל וזכאיס לחוק הסבות ככל עולה כארצות הגולה.

החלטה הסטורית זו פתחה פרק חדס בהסטוריה הארזכה סל יהודי אתיופיה העקובה כדס וקידוס הסט על עקרון יחוד הבורא ותורתנו הקדושה במסך כל הדורות. אולם גבורינו אלה לא לחינם מסרו את נפסם. כחופיב ע"י הגעגופיס אל ארץ האבות ולהיבת ציו בזמנים טעברו רבים היו הנסיונות טנעשו ע"י אבותינו לעלות ארצה בכוח עצמם. אולם כל מאסציהם עלו בתוהו. ועתה אם כי רחוקה עדיין הדרך ליציאתנו כמצריס כיון סאנו נמצאיב על הדרלאהחלמא דגאולה מרגיסים אנו דחף פנימי לברך " ברוך סהחינ" וקיימנוווהגיענו לזמן הזה". סעתה כל מאמצינו יחרכזו אך ורק למסרה אחת לבצוא את הדרכים אסר יובילולנו ארצה לפטן נקיים את דברי הנביא "וסבו בניה לגבולכ". כבצבר כן גם עתה סאיפתנו ורצוננו עזים לקטור את גורלנו יגודלו סל העם הטובן בציון להסתחף בבנין ארצנו הקדוסה ובהפרחת הסטבה ובעא צורך להגן עליה צדכנו.

כבוד ראש הממסלה,

אנו יהודיאתיופיה הפלסיס ראסי קהלותינו, זקנינו, כהנינוומורינו סהתקהלנו בכפר הברכזי כאוכבובר, הננו מביעיס.בזה את תודתנו לכבוד ראש הממסלה, לסרי הממסלה ולנת.גיבים הרוחניים סבדינה וכן לסוסדות ולאיסים באסר הם כם סעזרו לנו וחמכו בנו להגיע למעבד זה.

יהי רצון טבזבנך, כבוד ראס הממסלה, יחקיים בנו דברי הנביא "והיה ביום ההוא יוסיף ה' שנית ידו לקנות את שאר עמו אסר יסאר מאסור ומצמריכ ומפתרוס ומכוס ומעילב ומסנער וכחמת ומאי היס ונבא נס לגויים ואסף נדחי ישראל ונפצות יהודה יקבצ כארבע כנפות הארץ." אבן יהי רצון.

ח''חי מדינת ישראל לעולם!

קהילת בית-ישראל

בכבוד רב ובהערצה

נונדר בסם יהודי אתיופיה הפלסים
יונה בוגלה

A New Chapter in the Long History of Ethiopian Jewry

B"H

Ambover, 12th Sivan 5735 (May 22, 1975)

To His Eminence
Mr. Yitzhak Rabin
Prime Minister of Israel
Jerusalem, Israel

To the Honorable Prime Minister:

In the words of the prophet, "How beautiful upon the mountains are the feet of him that brings good tidings, that announces peace; that brings good tidings of good, that announces salvation…" (Isaiah 52:7). In recent weeks, we the Ethiopian Jews, The Falashas, were informed of a message issued by the government of Israel stating the decision to include the Ethiopian Jews, The Falashas, in the greater congregation of Israel, and that we are entitled to the right of the law of return just like any other immigrant from the Diaspora.

This historical decision opens a new chapter in the lengthy history of Ethiopian Jewry, a history full of bloodshed and sacred sacrifice on behalf of the principles of a single God and our holy Torah throughout many generations. However, these heroes of ours did not sacrifice their lives for nothing, their desperate longing for the land of our forefathers and their desire to return to Zion lives on. In days of yore, many attempts were made by our ancestors to make *aliya* to the land of Israel, however all of their efforts came to naught. Now, although there is still a long way to go before we will experience our own exodus from Egypt, given that we are standing at the start of the path towards redemption we feel a rather urgent inner need to make the blessing, "Blessed is the Lord who has kept us alive and sustained us and allowed us to live to see the present time." From this point on, all of our efforts will be focused on a single goal: To find the ways that will lead us to the Holy Land in order that we may be able to fulfill the words of the prophet, "…and the children shall return to their own border." (Jeremiah 31:16).

Honorable Prime Minister,

We, the Ethiopian Jews, The Falashas, through the heads of our communities, our elders, our priests and teachers, who have gathered in the central village of Ambover – would like to hereby express our gratitude to the officers of the government and the spiritual leaders of the state, as well as the organizations and individuals who have assisted us and supported us in achieving our present status.

May it be the will of the Lord, honorable Prime Minister, that we merit to fulfill the words of the prophet: "And it shall come to pass in that day, that the Lord shall set His hand again the second time to recover the remnant of His people, that shall be left, from Assyria, and from Egypt, from Pathros, and from Cush, and from Elam, and from Shinar, and from Hamat, and from the islands of the sea. And He shall set up a banner for the nations, and shall assemble the outcasts of Israel, and gather together the dispersed of Judah from the four corners of the earth." (Isaiah 11:11–12). Amen.

Long live the State of Israel, forever and ever!!
With great respect and admiration,
On behalf of the Ethiopian Jews, The Falashas,
[Yona Bogale and the Leaders of the Villages of Ambover and Seramle]

(Waldman, *From Ethiopia*, 212–213)

Rabban Gamliel used to say,
Anyone who has not pronounced
these three words on Pesaḥ,
has not done his duty.
And here they are:

רַבָּן גַּמְלִיאֵל הָיָה אוֹמֵר
כָּל שֶׁלֹּא אָמַר שְׁלוֹשָׁה דְבָרִים אֵלּוּ בַּפֶּסַח
לֹא יָצָא יְדֵי חוֹבָתוֹ
וְאֵלּוּ הֵן

פֶּסַח מַצָּה וּמָרוֹר
PESAḤ MATZA MAROR

פֶּסַח

שֶׁהָיוּ אֲבוֹתֵינוּ אוֹכְלִים בִּזְמַן שֶׁבֵּית הַמִּקְדָּשׁ הָיָה קַיָּם
עַל שׁוּם מָה
עַל שׁוּם שֶׁפָּסַח הַקָּדוֹשׁ בָּרוּךְ הוּא
עַל בָּתֵּי אֲבוֹתֵינוּ בְּמִצְרַיִם
שֶׁנֶּאֱמַר
וַאֲמַרְתֶּם זֶבַח־פֶּסַח הוּא לַיהוה
אֲשֶׁר פָּסַח עַל־בָּתֵּי בְנֵי־יִשְׂרָאֵל בְּמִצְרַיִם
בְּנָגְפּוֹ אֶת־מִצְרַיִם
וְאֶת־בָּתֵּינוּ הִצִּיל
וַיִּקֹּד הָעָם וַיִּשְׁתַּחֲווּ:

PESAḤ

the offering which our ancestors used to eat
as long as the Temple stood –
What is the reason for that?
It is because the Holy One,
blessed is He,
skipped over (PASAḤ)
the houses of our forefathers in Egypt,
as it is said:
"And you shall say it is the Pesaḥ sacrifice for the LORD,
who skipped over the houses of the children of Israel
in Egypt
when He smote Egypt,
and saved our houses.
And the people bowed down and worshiped."

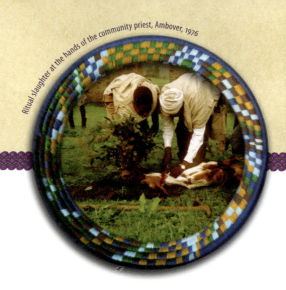

Ritual slaughter at the hands of the community priest, Ambover, 1976

THE SACRIFICIAL PRAYER

You showed favor to the sacrifice of Abel
So shall You receive our sacrifice.

You showed favor to the sacrifice of Elazar
You lent Your ear to David's prayer
So shall You hear our prayer, Lord.

In accordance with the priestly lineage of
Aaron
And the sacrifice of Abel
So shall our sacrifice be considered before
You.

We offer our sacrifice to You
You who deserve all praise;
Willingly accept the righteous offerings we
bring You
So that one day Your altar will be graced
By the return of the ritual sacrifices.

Offer up righteous offerings
Offer up fragrant sacrifices to the Lord,
I shall encircle Your altar, dear Lord,
In order to hear the sounds of Your praise.

Dear Lord, please shelter me in the shade
of Your wings.
Our dear Father, please shelter us in the
shade of Your wings.

May the offering of the righteous rise and
be accepted
And may its fragrance grace Your lofty
countenance.

The offering of the faithful servant of the
Lord,
The sacrifice for salvation.
The sacrificial flame is a guiding light.
The offering shall obtain forgiveness for our
sins.
The offering shall atone for our iniquities.
The offering shall put out the penitential
fires.
The sacrifice is pure and bears no blemish.

In the name of Aaron, the high priest at the
altar
And Moses, the greatest prophet of Israel.

And the Lord heeded the sacrifice of Abel
And beheld the prayer of David.

For the Lord accepted the sacrifice of Abel
And the prayer of David.

Accept our sacrifice like that of Abel.
Take this prayer from our lips like the
prayer of David.
The sacrifice shall bring peace,
For it is an offering to the Lord.

Who has made the sacrifice a goodly thing,
A treasured repository of life.

May the sacrifice rise unto the Lord God.

And the priests offered complete sacrifices, In accordance with the laws of the Lord God.

May this sacrifice rise before the lofty Lord.

May this sacrifice be as the Tree of Life in the Garden.

May the offering of the righteous illuminate like the sun.

May my sacrifices and offerings issue a pleasing fragrance before the Lord.

May the fat of the offering and every sacrifice flutter before the Lord as He beholds these offerings.

Even those offerings and sacrifices of the Sabbath, for the Lord God is One.

And the Lord saw and Abraham offered a sacrifice there to the Lord.

Passover sacrifice, Semien, 1950(?)

And David offered peace-offerings.

May the sacrifice be plentiful not meager.

May the glorious sacrifices speak on my behalf.

May the Lord gather His faithful to Him
Those who offer sacrifices to Him in accordance with the law.

Rise up to greet Me, O children of Israel,
With offerings and sacrifices in the House of the Lord.

Make your offerings before me, O children of Aaron,
With sacrifices and offerings in the House of the Lord.

Grant atonement to their souls, enrich those who offer them.

All sacrifices and offerings

Will then rise once more from Your sacred altar.

(Halévy, 25–28)

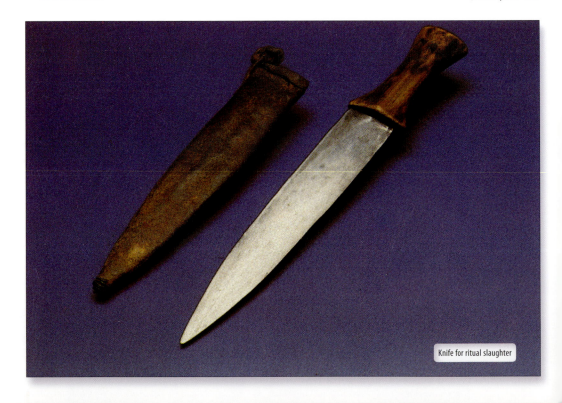

Knife for ritual slaughter

מַצָּה זוֹ

שֶׁאָנוּ אוֹכְלִים, עַל שׁוּם מָה

עַל שׁוּם שֶׁלֹּא הִסְפִּיק בְּצֵקָם שֶׁל אֲבוֹתֵינוּ לְהַחֲמִיץ

עַד שֶׁנִּגְלָה עֲלֵיהֶם מֶלֶךְ מַלְכֵי הַמְּלָכִים

הַקָּדוֹשׁ בָּרוּךְ הוּא, וּגְאָלָם

שֶׁנֶּאֱמַר

וַיֹּאפוּ אֶת־הַבָּצֵק אֲשֶׁר הוֹצִיאוּ מִמִּצְרַיִם

עֻגֹת מַצּוֹת, כִּי לֹא חָמֵץ

כִּי־גֹרְשׁוּ מִמִּצְרַיִם, וְלֹא יָכְלוּ לְהִתְמַהְמֵהַּ

וְגַם־צֵדָה לֹא־עָשׂוּ לָהֶם:

The matzot are now raised:

MATZA

which we eat – What is the reason for that?
It is because the dough which our fathers prepared,
did not manage to ferment before
He revealed Himself to them, the Supreme King of kings,
the Holy One, blessed is He, and redeemed them,
as it is said:
"And they baked the dough
which they brought out from Egypt
into unleavened cakes, because it was not fermented:
because they were driven out of Egypt,
and they could not delay,
nor had they prepared for themselves any provision."

Eating the matza along the synagogue façade, Uzava, 1963

Preparing lettuce to serve as bitter herbs, Addis Ababa, 1993

The bitter herb is now raised:

MAROR

which we eat – What is the reason for that?
It is because the Egyptians
embittered the lives of our forefathers in Egypt,
as it is said:
"And they made their lives bitter with hard bondage,
in mortar and in brick,
and in all manner of bondage in the field:
all their bondage wherein they made them serve was with rigor."

מגביה את המרור ואומר:

מָרוֹר זֶה

שֶׁאָנוּ אוֹכְלִים עַל שׁוּם מָה
עַל שׁוּם שֶׁמֵּרְרוּ הַמִּצְרִים אֶת חַיֵּי אֲבוֹתֵינוּ בְּמִצְרַיִם
שֶׁנֶּאֱמַר
וַיְמָרְרוּ אֶת־חַיֵּיהֶם בַּעֲבֹדָה קָשָׁה, בְּחֹמֶר וּבִלְבֵנִים
וּבְכָל־עֲבֹדָה בַּשָּׂדֶה
אֵת כָּל־עֲבֹדָתָם אֲשֶׁר־עָבְדוּ בָהֶם בְּפָרֶךְ:

We Have Arrived in the Garden of Eden and Emerged from the Darkness into Light and Freedom

Kes Abba Yitzchak, Atlit, 1985

Kes Abba Yitzchak, Atlit
21st Adar 5742 (March 16, 1982)

To the Honorable Prime Minister of Israel
Mr. Menachem Begin
Officials and Members of the Knesset

Re: Aliya of Falashas from Ethiopia

We, the Falashas, who were exiled in the darkness of Ethiopia, have now arrived in the Garden of Eden and emerged from the darkness into light and freedom. Because of you, Mr. Menachem Begin, we have arrived in the Holy Land, the land of Israel.

Just as the Lord spoke to his faithful servant Moses saying that the time had come for him to make his way to the land that had been promised to Abraham, Isaac and Jacob, so too the time has come for us to make our way to the Holy Land. I hope that I will soon get to see the Western Wall with my own eyes, that only remaining wall of the Holy Temple, and the government of Israel.

May it be that the Lord assist us and the government of Israel, just as He saved our leader Moses from the hands of the Egyptians, when the children of Israel were led out of slavery to freedom, and the sea split before them. In the same manner, you have saved us from the cruel hands of the rulers of Ethiopia. The moment that our feet touched the soil of the Holy Land, we were welcomed by all concerned and we have been warmly accepted and well-treated.

We offer our thanks to God Almighty and to the government of Israel as well. Please continue in your endeavors to ensure that all Ethiopian Jews might make their way to the land of Israel. I myself am an 83 year-old priest, and for 53 years I have been supporting Ethiopian Jewry in matters of religion, including *Nidda*, kashrut, festivals, circumcision, and weddings in accordance with the traditions of Moses and Jacob, etc. As of today I have in my possession a Torah scroll written in the Ge'ez language, as well as a collection of prayer books.

Dear Prime Minister, you are hereby invited to visit my home with all your entourage. When I would go to my Maker, my soul would be at peace knowing that I will be buried in the land that I have dreamt of my entire life. May Jerusalem, the cradle of our religion, live forever!

I have written this letter in the name of the entire Ethiopian Jewish community.

I would be greatly pleased to receive a reply in your own hand.

Priest Isaac Gudzan,
Absorption Center of Atlit
Fikadu Yimharen
Isaiah Zahariku

(Waldman, *From Ethiopia*, 218–220)

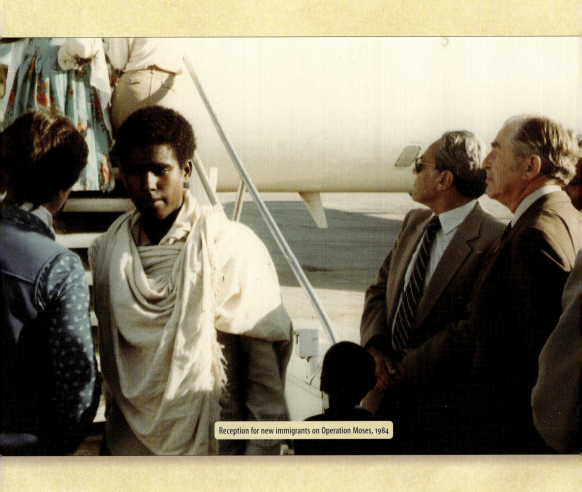

Reception for new immigrants on Operation Moses, 1984

At the absorption center for Olim on Operation Moses, Ashkelon, 1984

הַלְלוּיָהּ

הַלְלוּ עַבְדֵי יהוה, הַלְלוּ אֶת־שֵׁם יהוה:
יְהִי שֵׁם יהוה מְבֹרָךְ, מֵעַתָּה וְעַד־עוֹלָם:
מִמִּזְרַח־שֶׁמֶשׁ עַד־מְבוֹאוֹ, מְהֻלָּל שֵׁם יהוה:
רָם עַל־כָּל־גּוֹיִם יהוה, עַל הַשָּׁמַיִם כְּבוֹדוֹ:
מִי כַּיהוה אֱלֹהֵינוּ, הַמַּגְבִּיהִי לָשָׁבֶת:
הַמַּשְׁפִּילִי לִרְאוֹת, בַּשָּׁמַיִם וּבָאָרֶץ:
מְקִימִי מֵעָפָר דָּל, מֵאַשְׁפֹּת יָרִים אֶבְיוֹן:
לְהוֹשִׁיבִי עִם־נְדִיבִים, עִם נְדִיבֵי עַמּוֹ:
מוֹשִׁיבִי עֲקֶרֶת הַבַּיִת, אֵם־הַבָּנִים שְׂמֵחָה

הַלְלוּיָהּ:

HALLELUYA

Servants of the Lᴏʀᴅ, give praise; praise the name of the Lᴏʀᴅ.
Blessed be the name of the Lᴏʀᴅ now and for evermore.
From the rising of the sun to its setting, may the Lᴏʀᴅ's name be praised.
High is the Lᴏʀᴅ above all nations; His glory is above the heavens.
Who is like the Lᴏʀᴅ our God, who sits enthroned so high,
yet turns so low to see the heavens and the earth?
He raises the poor from the dust and the needy from the refuse heap,
giving them a place alongside princes, the princes of His people.
He makes the woman in a childless house a happy mother of children.

HALLELUYA

בְּצֵאת יִשְׂרָאֵל מִמִּצְרָיִם
בֵּית יַעֲקֹב מֵעַם לֹעֵז:

When Israel went out of Egypt,
the house of Jacob
from a people of strange language,

הָיְתָה יְהוּדָה לְקָדְשׁוֹ
יִשְׂרָאֵל מַמְשְׁלוֹתָיו:

Judah became His sanctuary,
Israel His dominion.

הַיָּם רָאָה וַיָּנֹס
הַיַּרְדֵּן יִסֹּב לְאָחוֹר:

The sea saw and fled;
the Jordan turned back.

הֶהָרִים רָקְדוּ כְאֵילִים
גְּבָעוֹת כִּבְנֵי־צֹאן:

The mountains skipped like rams,
the hills like lambs.

מַה־לְּךָ הַיָּם כִּי תָנוּס
הַיַּרְדֵּן תִּסֹּב לְאָחוֹר:

Why was it, sea, that you fled?
Jordan, why did you turn back?

הֶהָרִים תִּרְקְדוּ כְאֵילִים
גְּבָעוֹת כִּבְנֵי־צֹאן:

Why, mountains, did you skip like rams,
and you, hills, like lambs?

מִלִּפְנֵי אָדוֹן חוּלִי אָרֶץ
מִלִּפְנֵי אֱלוֹהַּ יַעֲקֹב:

It was at the presence of the LORD,
    Creator of the earth,
at the presence of the God of Jacob,

הַהֹפְכִי הַצּוּר אֲגַם־מָיִם
חַלָּמִישׁ לְמַעְיְנוֹ־מָיִם:

who turned the rock into a pool of water,
flint into a flowing spring.

◄ continue on page 128

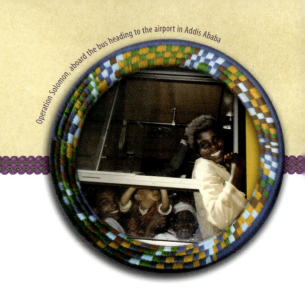
Operation Solomon, aboard the bus heading to the airport in Addis Ababa

HE SPLIT THE WATERS AND LED THE PEOPLE ACROSS

A Prayer for the Passover Holiday

He split the waters and led the people
   across
Stood the water to either side in columns
Guiding them in a cloud by day
And by a column of fiery light all through
   the night…
I fed them manna in the desert
For forty years in that very desert,
I bequeathed a bountiful land to them
That would flow for them with milk and
   honey
And provide them with ample wheat and
   wine.
The Lord spoke to me in His voice so holy
The Lord spoke to me with His voice so
   fine.

(*And You Shall Tell it to Your Children*, 17)

Operation Solomon, in front of the Israeli Embassy in Addis Ababa

Operation Solomon, aboard the bus heading to the airport in Addis Ababa

PRAISED BE THE NAME OF GOD WHO LED US OUT OF EGYPT

Blessed be the Lord God of Israel,
The Master of all flesh and spirit.

Rise up and stand tall
And bless the Lord our God
Now and forever,
Bless the praiseworthy name of
    His mighty glory
With every possible blessing.

Praise be unto the Lord our God.
    May it be His will, therefore,
That He bless us, and guard us, and show us
    compassion, for He is God.

We shall sing to the Lord that He might
    shine His light upon us,
And erase all our sins.

We shall bless the Lord for He is great
And deserving of praise throughout the
    generations
And forever after.

May the Lord remember us and bless us,
Bless the House of Israel
And bless the House of Aaron.

Registration of Olim at the Israel Embassy in Addis Ababa, 1991

Operation Solomon

Bless us all,
Bless them all,
Those who fear
The Lord God,
The young
And old alike.

May the Lord increase you
And your children,
You shall be blessed before the Lord
Who created heaven
And earth.

The heavens belong to the Lord
And the earth was given over
To humanity.

The dead cannot sing your praises,
O Lord,
Nor those who are silenced forever in the
    earth.

We, the living
Shall bless the Lord now and forever.

For the Lord has satisfied the starving soul
And fed the hungry spirit with all good
    things.

May the name of the Lord be praised
He who redeemed us from Egypt down to
    this very day,
May the name of the Lord be praised now,
And be well-founded forever.

Praise be to the Lord now and forever,
Amen.

May my oaths resound before the Lord and
    succor me,
For the Lord needs none to assist Him.

And it was said: O Master
Who shall live forever,
Who shall watch over all
From His Jerusalem in heaven,
You reside in the heavens,
And Your throne shall never be conquered
    by any enemy,
Your praise is never-ending.
His angels shall rise in awe,
And they shall stand and be given life in
    heaven through my commandments.

Your voice is mighty
And Your words everlasting
And Your voice, Your Commandments and
    Your Law
Shall never cease.

Your commandments are awesome
And the fine depths of Your laws shall never
    be eradicated.

Your anger shall determine the very fate of
    mountains,

And Your name is righteous forever and
    ever,
Amen.

Lend Your ear to the prayer of Your faithful
    servant.

Halleluya, Lord, Halleluya.

(*Eshkoli*, 133–134)

Attending to the Matter of Their Jewishness and Exodus to Israel

14th Iyar 5751 (April 28, 1991)

For the Attention of
The Chief Rabbis of Israel,
May They be Granted Long Life

Greetings and salutations,

We, the spiritual leaders of the Ethiopian Jewish community (the Kessim), are greatly concerned about the physical condition of our brethren in Addis Ababa, due to the new situation that has arisen in the country – in particular, we are concerned about the condition of those who have been taken forcibly (the Falash Mura). We are extremely worried that they might fall victim to the security situation that has developed within Ethiopia.

Therefore, we the undersigned hereby request from the honorable Chief Rabbis of Israel – may they be granted long life – that they send representatives urgently to verify the Jewish origin of those taken forcibly and to assist them in making *aliya* to the land of Israel.

[Eight signatures of Kessim from the greater community with the signature of the Chief Rabbi of the Ethiopian Jewry in Israel]

(M.W.A)

Making *aliya* – between Atzede Mariam and Gondar, 1991

ב"ה, י"ד אייר, תנש"א

לכבוד

מרן הרבנים הראשיים לישראל שליט"א

שלום וברכה,

אנחנו המנהיגים הרוחניים של יהודי אתיופיה (הקסים), מאוד
מודאגים ממצב מצבם הפיזי של אחינו באדיס אבבה, בגלל המצב החדש
באתיופיה, במיוחד על מצב האנוסים (פלסמורה), אנו מאוד חוששים
שלא יהיו קורבן במצב הביטחוני שנוצר בתוך אתיופיה.

לפיכך אנו החתומים מטה מבקשים מכבוד הרבנים הראשיים לישראל
שליט"א לשֹ לוח בדחיפות אנשים מטעמכם כדי לטפל בעניין יהדותם,
ועליהם ארצה.

The Dry Bones

Funeral, Ambover, 1976

Tadese Wondem, As Related to a Delegation from the State of Israel Inspecting the Matter of the Falash Mura

Chohit, 12th Iyar 5752
(May 15, 1992)

We are brothers. We are part of the tribe, the nation, and we wish to join the rest of our people. If you wish to, you can take us to our children, and if you will not, then we will have no choice but to sit and wait. It is written in the books of the prophets that the time will come when the government of Israel will bring even the dry bones of the nation of Israel home, and not just the living. We are the dry bones of the Jewish people.

(M.W.A)

Kes Taye, right before making *aliya* to Israel, with a knife for ritual slaughter of sacrifices in his case, along with the ashes of a red heifer, Addis Ababa, 1992

The Time Has Come to Return to Jerusalem

Making *aliya* to Israel, 1992

Feleka Asayehen, Tamergot,
18th Iyar 5752 (May 21, 1992)

When the nation of Israel was exiled in the times of Isaiah, Jeremiah and Daniel, the Lord spoke through His prophets, saying: "You shall return to your homeland, to Jerusalem."

They asked Him: "When? How?"

And the Lord answered, saying: "When you shall see a comet in the four corners of heaven it will be a sign that the time has come for the nation of Israel to return to its homeland."

The time has come. The Jews of Ethiopia traveled on foot for months, they were tortured and murdered, they went through hell and, nevertheless, they reached Jerusalem. Behold the fact that your automobile, from the Israeli embassy, has made its way all the way here. The comet shall drag us all along to Jerusalem. We are a part of the Jewish people and the time has come for us to return to Jerusalem.

When I see you, the representatives of the State of Israel, here in this very village of mine, I feel like I have arrived in the Garden of Eden. I do not know if I will merit to arrive in the land of Israel, however I am certain that, with the help of God, my children and grandchildren shall make *aliya* to the Holy Land.

(M.W.A)

Tamergot, 1992

Prayer, Gondar, 2001

HE SHALL BE THE LORD

The Lord, the great, and mighty one,
    he shall be the Lord

Who has brought me to this day,
To this very day

He shall be the Lord

The Lord who has not forgotten me
    to this day,
To this very day,

He shall be the Lord

Who shall see the bounty?
Who will be granted long life,

He shall be the mighty Lord…

(*And You Shall Tell It to Your Children*, 13)

Transfer from the aliya office in Gondar to the Olim camp in Teda, 1992

Blessed are You, LORD our God, King of the Universe,
who has redeemed us,
and redeemed our fathers from Egypt,
and has brought us safely to this night
on which we eat matza and maror:
likewise, O LORD our God, and God of our fathers,
grant that we may live to celebrate
many other festivals and holy days,
coming peacefully on their way to meet us;
that we may have the joy of rebuilding Your city,
and the delight of witnessing Your Temple service:
and that we may eat there of the festive sacrifices,
and of the Pesaḥ sacrifices,*
whose blood is sprinkled on the wall of Your altar for favor.
And we shall thankfully
sing a new song for our redemption
and for the salvation of our souls.
Blessed are You, O God, who has redeemed Israel.

On Motza'ei Shabbat, some say
"of the Pesah sacrifices and of the festive sacrifices."

I am hereby prepared and ready to fulfill the commandment of the second of the four cups. For the sake of the unification of the Holy One, blessed be He, and His Divine Presence, through that which is hidden and concealed, in the name of all Israel.

Blessed are You, LORD our God, King of the Universe,
who creates the produce of the vine.

Drink while reclining to the left.

בָּרוּךְ אַתָּה יהוה אֱלֹהֵינוּ מֶלֶךְ הָעוֹלָם

אֲשֶׁר גְּאָלָנוּ, וְגָאַל אֶת אֲבוֹתֵינוּ מִמִּצְרַיִם

וְהִגִּיעָנוּ הַלַּיְלָה הַזֶּה, לֶאֱכָל בּוֹ מַצָּה וּמָרוֹר.

כֵּן יהוה אֱלֹהֵינוּ וֵאלֹהֵי אֲבוֹתֵינוּ

יַגִּיעֵנוּ לְמוֹעֲדִים וְלִרְגָלִים אֲחֵרִים

הַבָּאִים לִקְרָאתֵנוּ לְשָׁלוֹם

שְׂמֵחִים בְּבִנְיַן עִירֶךָ

וְשָׂשִׂים בַּעֲבוֹדָתֶךָ

וְנֹאכַל שָׁם

מִן הַזְּבָחִים וּמִן הַפְּסָחִים*

אֲשֶׁר יַגִּיעַ דָּמָם

עַל קִיר מִזְבַּחֲךָ לְרָצוֹן

וְנוֹדֶה לְךָ

שִׁיר חָדָשׁ

עַל גְּאֻלָּתֵנוּ וְעַל פְּדוּת נַפְשֵׁנוּ

בָּרוּךְ אַתָּה יהוה, גָּאַל יִשְׂרָאֵל.

במוצאי שבת, יש האומרים: "מִן הַפְּסָחִים וּמִן הַזְּבָחִים."

הנני מוכן ומזומן לקיים מצוות כוס שני של ארבע כוסות.
לשם ייחוד קודשא בריך הוא ושכינתיה על ידי ההוא טמיר ונעלם בשם כל ישראל.

בָּרוּךְ אַתָּה יהוה אֱלֹהֵינוּ מֶלֶךְ הָעוֹלָם, בּוֹרֵא פְּרִי הַגָּפֶן.

שותים בהסבת שמאל.

129

Receive Us with Your Blessing as Jews

Consecration of a new Torah Scroll, Ambover, 1975

Addis Ababa, 15th of Av 5753
(August 2, 1993)

For the Attention of
The Honorable Chief Rabbi of Israel
Rabbi Meir Lau
And the Honorable Chief Rabbi of Israel,
Leader of Zion,
Rabbi Bakshi-Doron
The Chief Rabbinate of Israel
Jerusalem

We are Jews numbering 4,000 waiting to be rescued. We respectfully write to you and to all members of the Chief Rabbinate Council this letter hoping that our fate is in your hands.

In the beginning with the help of NACOEJ, we were teaching and learning ourselves by forming study groups the history, culture and the faith of Jewishness. Later on we studied the laws of Pessah by making a large Seder for all 4,000 people with the help and leadership and guidance of Rabbi Waldman. Recently

with our request, we were learning and studying Jewish faith, history and culture of Israel and morning and afternoon services (praying) were done by the help of again by our brother Rabbi Waldman. Still we do not stop the study groups and the services.

We will follow the laws of Aliyah and will do what the Chief Rabbinate order or advise us to do.

Last but not least accept our repentance and welcome us as Jews and assist us in our rapid return to the land of Israel and live freely as Jews.

Thank you,
Representatives of the Community
[12 signatures – Ed.]

(M.W.A.)

Consecration of a new Torah Scroll, Addis Ababa, 1993

August 2, 1993

OFFICE OF THE CHIEF RABINAT OF ISRAEL   02- 231899

To HONORABLE CHIEF RABBI ELIYAHU BAKSHI DORON
JERUSALEM

WE ARE JEWS Numbering 4,000 WAITING to b
Rescued. We RESPECTFULLY WRITE TO you AND TO ALL members of
THE CHIEF RABINAT COUNCIL THIS LETTER Hoping THAT OUR FATE
IS IN YOUR HANDS.

IN THE BEGINING WITH THE HELP OF NACOEJ, WE
WERE TEACHING AND LEARNING OUR SELVES by forming STUDY Groups
THE HISTORY, CULTURE AND THE FAITH OF JEWISHNESS. LATER on
WE STUDIED THE LAWS of PESSAH BY MAKING A LARGE SED
FOR ALL 4000 PEOPLE WITH THE HELP AND LEDERSHIP AND
Guidance of RABBI WALDMAN. RECENTLEY WITH OUR
REQUESETION, WE WERE LEARNING AND STUDYING JEWISH
FAITH, HISTORY and culture of ISRAEL AND MORNING AND
AFTERNOON SERVICES (PRAYING) WERE done by THE HELP of
Again By OUR BroTher RABBI WALDMAN. STILL we do not
stop the study groups and the services.

WE WILL FOLLOW THE LAWS OF ALIYAH AND WILL DO
WHAT THE CHIEF RABBINATE ORDER OR ADVICE US TO DO.

LAST BUT NOT LEAST ACCEPT OUR REPENTANCE
AND WELCOME US AS JEWS AND ASSIST US IN OUR RAPID
RETURN TO THE LAND OF ISRAEL AND LIVE Freely AS JEWS.

THANK you

REPRESENTATIVES OF THE community

1) DEGU ABUNIE
2) MALEDE AYANAW
3) TESFA TAREKEGNE
4) ALEKEGNE ASMAMAW
5) FEKADU GESSE
6) AGEGNEHU KASSA

7) NAGA ALENE
8) REDA DETALE
9) BIRARA ENDALE
10) GENET DEGU
11) Wubalech ALEMU
12) TSEGAW ADMASE

חיים • **רחצה**   נוטלים את הידיים לסעודה ומברכים:

בָּרוּךְ אַתָּה יהוה אֱלֹהֵינוּ מֶלֶךְ הָעוֹלָם
אֲשֶׁר קִדְּשָׁנוּ בְּמִצְוֹתָיו, וְצִוָּנוּ עַל נְטִילַת יָדֶיִם.

WASHING THE HANDS

In preparation for the meal, all participants wash their hands and recite the blessing:

Blessed are You, Lord our God, King of the Universe,
who has made us holy through His commandments,
and has commanded us about washing hands.

Preparing the matza, Wolleka, 1984

GIVE US SUSTENANCE

By the merits of the twelve tribes,
The fifteen prophets,
Ninety-nine angels
Ancestors and forefathers,
O Lord, Keeper of the heavens
And Creator of the earth,
Give us sustenance.

(Halévy, *Agau*, 180–181)

THE BLESSING OVER BREAD

Give praise and thanks to the Lord and His
   attending angels,
May the name of the Lord be praised
   forever
And may the Lord grant us the blessings
   given to our forefathers,
Abraham, Isaac and Jacob,
And may these blessings bring us only good,
May it thus be the will of the Lord,
   Amen […]

(Identity and Tradition, 67)

osh Hashanah prayers in Gondar, 2008

הִנְנִי מוּכָן וּמְזוּמָּן לְקַיֵּם מִצְוַות אֲכִילַת מַצָּה.
לְשֵׁם יִחוּד קוּדְשָׁא בְּרִיךְ הוּא וּשְׁכִינְתֵּיהּ עַל יְדֵי הַהוּא טָמִיר וְנֶעְלָם בְּשֵׁם כָּל יִשְׂרָאֵל.

בָּרוּךְ אַתָּה יהוה אֱלֹהֵינוּ מֶלֶךְ הָעוֹלָם, הַמּוֹצִיא לֶחֶם מִן הָאָרֶץ.

מניח את המצה התחתונה מידו ואוחז את העליונה ואת האמצעית ומברך:

בָּרוּךְ אַתָּה יהוה אֱלֹהֵינוּ מֶלֶךְ הָעוֹלָם
אֲשֶׁר קִדְּשָׁנוּ בְּמִצְוֹתָיו, וְצִוָּנוּ עַל אֲכִילַת מַצָּה.

נוטל לעצמו ונותן לכל אחד מן המסובים כזית מן המצה העליונה
וכזית מן האמצעית, ואוכלים בהסבת שמאל.

BLESSINGS OVER THE THREE MATZOT

The leader holds all three matzot and recites:

I am hereby prepared and ready to fulfill the commandment of eating the matza.
For the sake of the unification of the Holy One, blessed be He, and His Divine Presence, through that which is hidden and concealed, in the name of all Israel.

Blessed are You, LORD our God, King of the Universe,
who brings forth bread from the earth.

The lowermost matza is replaced.
The leader recites the following blessing while holding the uppermost and middle matzot:

Blessed are You, LORD our God, King of the Universe,
who has made us holy through His commandments,
and has commanded us to eat matza.

*A piece of the uppermost matza, together with a piece of the middle matza,
is given to each member of the company. Eat while reclining to the left.*

Preparing the matza, Gondar, 2008

מרור • ᎯᎤᎾ ᏕᎹᎾ   נוטל כזית מרור לעצמו ולכל המסובים וטובלו בחרוסת:

הנני מוכן ומזומן לקיים מצוות אכילת מרור.

לשם ייחוד קודשא בריך הוא ושכינתיה על ידי ההוא טמיר ונעלם בשם כל ישראל.

בָּרוּךְ אַתָּה יהוה אֱלֹהֵינוּ מֶלֶךְ הָעוֹלָם
אֲשֶׁר קִדְּשָׁנוּ בְּמִצְוֹתָיו, וְצִוָּנוּ עַל אֲכִילַת מָרוֹר.

כורך • ᎶᎲᏆᎸᎸ   בוצע את המצה התחתונה, נוטל ממנה כזית
וכורך עמה כזית מן המרור, מחלק למסובים
(או שכל אחד מהם נוטל מן המצה השמורה שלפניו וכורך) ואומר:

זֵכֶר לַמִּקְדָּשׁ כְּהִלֵּל.
כֵּן עָשָׂה הִלֵּל בִּזְמַן שֶׁבֵּית הַמִּקְדָּשׁ הָיָה קַיָּם
הָיָה כּוֹרֵךְ פֶּסַח, מַצָּה וּמָרוֹר, וְאוֹכֵל בְּיַחַד
לְקַיֵּם מַה שֶׁנֶּאֱמַר: עַל־מַצּוֹת וּמְרֹרִים יֹאכְלֻהוּ:

אוכלים בהסבת שמאל.

EATING THE BITTER HERB

The maror is dipped in the ḥaroset before it is eaten.

I am hereby prepared and ready to fulfill the commandment of eating the maror.
For the sake of the unification of the Holy One, blessed be He, and His Divine Presence, through that which is hidden and concealed, in the name of all Israel.

Blessed are You, LORD our God, King of the Universe,
who has made us holy through His commandments,
and has commanded us to eat the bitter herb.

THE "SANDWICH"

Bitter herbs are sandwiched between two pieces of matza taken from the lowermost matza.

In commemoration of the Temple by Hillel:
During the Temple period he used to eat of the Pesaḥ lamb,
the matza and the maror all together,
in accordance with the biblical verse:
…and eat it (the Pesaḥ lamb) with matza and bitter herbs.

Eat while reclining to the left.

The festive meal is now eaten.

Students of the Jewish Agency seminar with the emissary Judah Sivan and Yona Bogale, Asmara, 1956

In the hold of the ship named *Bat Galim* on the way from the coast of Sudan to Sharm el-Sheikh, 1981

THE HIDDEN PORTION

*At the end of the meal, the remaining piece of the middle matza
which had been hidden earlier (the Afikoman), is eaten.*

I am hereby prepared and ready to fulfill the commandment of eating the Afikoman.
For the sake of the unification of the Holy One, blessed be He, and His Divine Presence,
through that which is hidden and concealed, in the name of all Israel.

פ״ח • **צפון**   בגמר הסעודה מוציא את פרוסת המצה שהצפין לאפיקומן,
נוטל כשני זיתים ונותן גם למסובים (או שהם נוטלים מן המצה השמורה שלפניהם), ואומרים:

הנני מוכן ומזומן לקיים מצוות אכילת אפיקומן.
לשם ייחוד קודשא בריך הוא ושכינתיה
על ידי ההוא טמיר ונעלם בשם כל ישראל.

GRACE AFTER MEALS

The third cup of wine is poured. The leader raises the cup and recites:

I am hereby prepared and ready to fulfill the positive commandment of Grace after Meals.
As it is written in the Torah:
"And you shall eat and be satisfied and bless the LORD your God,
  for the good land which He has given you."
For the sake of the unification of the Holy One, blessed be He,
  and His Divine Presence, through that which is hidden and concealed, in the name of all Israel.

A SONG OF ASCENTS.

When the LORD brought back the exiles of Zion,
  we were like people who dream.
Then were our mouths filled with laughter,
  and our tongues with songs of joy.
Then was it said among the nations,
"The LORD has done great things for them."
The LORD did do great things for us and we rejoiced.
Bring back our exiles, LORD, like streams in a dry land.
May those who sowed in tears, reap in joy.
May one who goes out weeping, carrying a bag of seed,
come back with songs of joy, carrying his sheaves.

Some add:
My mouth shall speak the praise of God,
and all creatures shall bless His holy name for ever and all time.
We will bless God now and for ever. Halleluya!
Thank the LORD for He is good: His loving-kindness is for ever.
Who can tell of the LORD's mighty acts and make all His praise be heard?

When three adult males are present, the leader announces:
Gentlemen: Let us say Grace.

May the name of the LORD be blessed from now on and forever.

May the name of the LORD be blessed from now on and forever.

With your permission, (my father and teacher / my mother and teacher / the Kohanim present
          / our teacher the Rabbi / the master of this house / the mistress of this house)
my masters and teachers,
we will now bless Him (*In a minyan:* our God)
of whose bounty we have eaten.

Blessed is He (*In a minyan:* our God) of whose bounty we have eaten
and by whose goodness we live.

Blessed is He (*In a minyan:* our God) of whose bounty we have eaten
and by whose goodness we live.
Blessed is He, and blessed is His name.

מוזגים כוס שלישי יש הנוטלים מים אחרונים. עורך הסדר אוחז את הכוס בימינו ואומר:

הנני מוכן ומזומן לקיים מצוות עשה של ברכת המזון,
כמו שכתוב בתורה
ואכלת ושבעת וברכת את יהוה אלהיך
על הארץ הטובה אשר נתן לך.
לשם יחוד קודשא בריך הוא ושכינתיה על ידי ההוא
טמיר ונעלם בשם כל ישראל.

שִׁיר הַמַּעֲלוֹת

בְּשׁוּב יהוה אֶת־שִׁיבַת צִיּוֹן, הָיִינוּ כְּחֹלְמִים:
אָז יִמָּלֵא שְׂחוֹק פִּינוּ וּלְשׁוֹנֵנוּ רִנָּה
אָז יֹאמְרוּ בַגּוֹיִם הִגְדִּיל יהוה לַעֲשׂוֹת עִם־אֵלֶּה:
הִגְדִּיל יהוה לַעֲשׂוֹת עִמָּנוּ, הָיִינוּ שְׂמֵחִים:
שׁוּבָה יהוה אֶת־שְׁבִיתֵנוּ, כַּאֲפִיקִים בַּנֶּגֶב:
הַזֹּרְעִים בְּדִמְעָה, בְּרִנָּה יִקְצֹרוּ:
הָלוֹךְ יֵלֵךְ וּבָכֹה נֹשֵׂא מֶשֶׁךְ־הַזָּרַע
בֹּא־יָבֹא בְרִנָּה נֹשֵׂא אֲלֻמֹּתָיו:

יש מוסיפים:

תְּהִלַּת יהוה יְדַבֶּר פִּי, וִיבָרֵךְ כָּל־בָּשָׂר שֵׁם קָדְשׁוֹ לְעוֹלָם וָעֶד:
וַאֲנַחְנוּ נְבָרֵךְ יָהּ מֵעַתָּה וְעַד־עוֹלָם, הַלְלוּיָהּ:
הוֹדוּ לַיהוה כִּי־טוֹב, כִּי לְעוֹלָם חַסְדּוֹ:
מִי יְמַלֵּל גְּבוּרוֹת יהוה, יַשְׁמִיעַ כָּל־תְּהִלָּתוֹ:

שלושה שאכלו כאחד חייבים לזמן:

רַבּוֹתַי, נְבָרֵךְ.

יְהִי שֵׁם יהוה מְבֹרָךְ מֵעַתָּה וְעַד־עוֹלָם:

יְהִי שֵׁם יהוה מְבֹרָךְ מֵעַתָּה וְעַד־עוֹלָם:

בִּרְשׁוּת (אָבִי מוֹרִי / אִמִּי מוֹרָתִי / כֹּהֲנִים / מוֹרֵנוּ הָרַב /
בַּעַל הַבַּיִת הַזֶּה / בַּעֲלַת הַבַּיִת הַזֶּה)

מָרָנָן וְרַבָּנָן וְרַבּוֹתַי נְבָרֵךְ (במניין: אֱלֹהֵינוּ) שֶׁאָכַלְנוּ מִשֶּׁלּוֹ.

בָּרוּךְ (במניין: אֱלֹהֵינוּ) שֶׁאָכַלְנוּ מִשֶּׁלּוֹ וּבְטוּבוֹ חָיִינוּ.

בָּרוּךְ (במניין: אֱלֹהֵינוּ) שֶׁאָכַלְנוּ מִשֶּׁלּוֹ וּבְטוּבוֹ חָיִינוּ.
בָּרוּךְ הוּא וּבָרוּךְ שְׁמוֹ.

BLESSED are You, Lord our God, King of the Universe,
who in His goodness feeds the whole world
with grace, kindness and compassion.
He gives food to all living things,
for His kindness is for ever.
Because of His continual great goodness,
we have never lacked food;
nor may we ever lack it,
for the sake of His great name.
For He is God who feeds and sustains all,
does good to all,
and prepares food for all creatures He has created.
Blessed are You, O Lord, who feeds all.

LET US GIVE THANKS TO YOU, Lord our God,
for having granted as a heritage to our ancestors,
a desirable, good and spacious land;
for bringing us out, Lord our God,
from the land of Egypt
freeing us from the house of slavery;
for Your covenant which You sealed in our flesh;
for Your Torah which You taught us;
for Your laws which You made known to us;
for the life, grace and kindness You have bestowed on us;
and for the food by which You continually feed and sustain us,
every day, every season, every hour .

For all this, O Lord our God,
we thank and bless You.
May Your name be blessed continually
by the mouth of all that lives, for ever and all time –
for so it is written: "You will eat and be satisfied, then you shall
bless the Lord your God for the good land He has given you."
Blessed are You, O Lord,
for the land and for the food.

HAVE COMPASSION, please, Lord our God,
on Israel Your people,
on Jerusalem Your city,
on Zion the dwelling place of Your glory,
on the royal house of David Your anointed,
and on the great and holy House that bears Your name.

בָּרוּךְ אַתָּה יהוה אֱלֹהֵינוּ מֶלֶךְ הָעוֹלָם
הַזָּן אֶת הָעוֹלָם כֻּלּוֹ בְּטוּבוֹ בְּחֵן בְּחֶסֶד וּבְרַחֲמִים
הוּא נוֹתֵן לֶחֶם לְכָל בָּשָׂר כִּי לְעוֹלָם חַסְדּוֹ.
וּבְטוּבוֹ הַגָּדוֹל, תָּמִיד לֹא חָסַר לָנוּ
וְאַל יֶחְסַר לָנוּ מָזוֹן לְעוֹלָם וָעֶד
בַּעֲבוּר שְׁמוֹ הַגָּדוֹל.
כִּי הוּא אֵל זָן וּמְפַרְנֵס לַכֹּל וּמֵטִיב לַכֹּל
וּמֵכִין מָזוֹן לְכָל בְּרִיּוֹתָיו אֲשֶׁר בָּרָא.
בָּרוּךְ אַתָּה יהוה, הַזָּן אֶת הַכֹּל.

נוֹדֶה לְּךָ יהוה אֱלֹהֵינוּ
עַל שֶׁהִנְחַלְתָּ לַאֲבוֹתֵינוּ
אֶרֶץ חֶמְדָּה טוֹבָה וּרְחָבָה
וְעַל שֶׁהוֹצֵאתָנוּ יהוה אֱלֹהֵינוּ מֵאֶרֶץ מִצְרַיִם
וּפְדִיתָנוּ מִבֵּית עֲבָדִים
וְעַל בְּרִיתְךָ שֶׁחָתַמְתָּ בִּבְשָׂרֵנוּ
וְעַל תּוֹרָתְךָ שֶׁלִּמַּדְתָּנוּ
וְעַל חֻקֶּיךָ שֶׁהוֹדַעְתָּנוּ
וְעַל חַיִּים חֵן וָחֶסֶד שֶׁחוֹנַנְתָּנוּ
וְעַל אֲכִילַת מָזוֹן שָׁאַתָּה זָן וּמְפַרְנֵס אוֹתָנוּ תָּמִיד
בְּכָל יוֹם וּבְכָל עֵת וּבְכָל שָׁעָה.

וְעַל הַכֹּל, יהוה אֱלֹהֵינוּ
אֲנַחְנוּ מוֹדִים לָךְ וּמְבָרְכִים אוֹתָךְ
יִתְבָּרַךְ שִׁמְךָ בְּפִי כָּל חַי תָּמִיד לְעוֹלָם וָעֶד
כַּכָּתוּב: וְאָכַלְתָּ וְשָׂבָעְתָּ, וּבֵרַכְתָּ אֶת־יהוה אֱלֹהֶיךָ
עַל־הָאָרֶץ הַטֹּבָה אֲשֶׁר נָתַן־לָךְ:
בָּרוּךְ אַתָּה יהוה, עַל הָאָרֶץ וְעַל הַמָּזוֹן.

רַחֶם נָא יהוה אֱלֹהֵינוּ
עַל יִשְׂרָאֵל עַמֶּךָ
וְעַל יְרוּשָׁלַיִם עִירֶךָ
וְעַל צִיּוֹן מִשְׁכַּן כְּבוֹדֶךָ
וְעַל מַלְכוּת בֵּית דָּוִד מְשִׁיחֶךָ
וְעַל הַבַּיִת הַגָּדוֹל וְהַקָּדוֹשׁ שֶׁנִּקְרָא שִׁמְךָ עָלָיו.

Our God, our Father,
tend us, feed us, sustain us and support us, relieve us and send us relief.
Lᴏʀᴅ our God, swiftly from all our troubles.
Please, Lᴏʀᴅ our God,
do not make us dependent on the gifts or loans of other people,
but only on Your full, open, holy and generous hand
so that we may suffer neither shame nor humiliation for ever and all time.

On Shabbat add: **FAVOR US,** Favor and strengthen us, Lᴏʀᴅ our God,
         through Your commandments,
         especially through the commandment of the seventh day,
         this great and holy Sabbath.
         For it is, for You, a great and holy day.
         On it we cease work and rest in love
         in accord with Your will's commandment.
         May it be Your will, Lᴏʀᴅ our God,
         to grant us rest without distress,
         grief, or lament on our day of rest.
         May You show us the consolation of Zion Your city,
         and the rebuilding of Jerusalem Your holy city,
         for You are the Master of salvation and consolation..

OUR GOD AND GOD OF OUR ANCESTORS,
may there rise, come, reach, appear, be favored, heard, regarded
and remembered before You, our recollection and remembrance,
as well as the remembrance of our ancestors,
and of the Messiah son of David Your servant,
and of Jerusalem Your holy city,
and of all Your people the house of Israel –
for deliverance and well-being, grace, loving-kindness and compassion,
life and peace, on this day of Festival of Matzot.
On it remember us, Lᴏʀᴅ our God, for good;
recollect us for blessing, and deliver us for life.
In accord with Your promise of salvation and compassion,
spare us and be gracious to us;
have compassion on us and deliver us,
for our eyes are turned to You because You are God,
gracious and compassionate.

A nd may Jerusalem the holy city be rebuilt soon, in our time.
Blessed are You, O Lᴏʀᴅ, who in His compassion will rebuild Jerusalem. Amen.

אֱלֹהֵינוּ, אָבִינוּ

רְעֵנוּ, זוּנֵנוּ, פַּרְנְסֵנוּ וְכַלְכְּלֵנוּ

וְהַרְוִיחֵנוּ, וְהַרְוַח לָנוּ יהוה אֱלֹהֵינוּ מְהֵרָה מִכָּל צָרוֹתֵינוּ.

וְנָא אַל תַּצְרִיכֵנוּ, יהוה אֱלֹהֵינוּ

לֹא לִידֵי מַתְּנַת בָּשָׂר וָדָם

וְלֹא לִידֵי הַלְוָאָתָם

כִּי אִם לְיָדְךָ הַמְּלֵאָה, הַפְּתוּחָה, הַקְּדוֹשָׁה וְהָרְחָבָה

שֶׁלֹּא נֵבוֹשׁ וְלֹא נִכָּלֵם לְעוֹלָם וָעֶד.

בשבת מוסיפים: **רְצֵה** וְהַחֲלִיצֵנוּ, יהוה אֱלֹהֵינוּ, בְּמִצְוֹתֶיךָ

וּבְמִצְוַת יוֹם הַשְּׁבִיעִי הַשַּׁבָּת הַגָּדוֹל וְהַקָּדוֹשׁ הַזֶּה

כִּי יוֹם זֶה גָּדוֹל וְקָדוֹשׁ הוּא לְפָנֶיךָ

לִשְׁבָּת בּוֹ, וְלָנוּחַ בּוֹ בְּאַהֲבָה כְּמִצְוַת רְצוֹנֶךָ

וּבִרְצוֹנְךָ הָנַח לָנוּ, יהוה אֱלֹהֵינוּ

שֶׁלֹּא תְהֵא צָרָה וְיָגוֹן וַאֲנָחָה בְּיוֹם מְנוּחָתֵנוּ

וְהַרְאֵנוּ, יהוה אֱלֹהֵינוּ, בְּנֶחָמַת צִיּוֹן עִירֶךָ

וּבְבִנְיַן יְרוּשָׁלַיִם עִיר קָדְשֶׁךָ

כִּי אַתָּה הוּא בַּעַל הַיְשׁוּעוֹת וּבַעַל הַנֶּחָמוֹת.

אֱלֹהֵינוּ וֵאלֹהֵי אֲבוֹתֵינוּ

יַעֲלֶה וְיָבוֹא וְיַגִּיעַ, וְיֵרָאֶה וְיֵרָצֶה וְיִשָּׁמַע, וְיִפָּקֵד

וְיִזָּכֵר זִכְרוֹנֵנוּ וּפִקְדוֹנֵנוּ, וְזִכְרוֹן אֲבוֹתֵינוּ

וְזִכְרוֹן מָשִׁיחַ בֶּן דָּוִד עַבְדֶּךָ

וְזִכְרוֹן יְרוּשָׁלַיִם עִיר קָדְשֶׁךָ

וְזִכְרוֹן כָּל עַמְּךָ בֵּית יִשְׂרָאֵל

לְפָנֶיךָ, לִפְלֵיטָה לְטוֹבָה, לְחֵן וּלְחֶסֶד וּלְרַחֲמִים

לְחַיִּים וּלְשָׁלוֹם בְּיוֹם

חַג הַמַּצּוֹת הַזֶּה.

זָכְרֵנוּ יהוה אֱלֹהֵינוּ בּוֹ לְטוֹבָה

וּפָקְדֵנוּ בוֹ לִבְרָכָה

וְהוֹשִׁיעֵנוּ בוֹ לְחַיִּים.

וּבִדְבַר יְשׁוּעָה וְרַחֲמִים, חוּס וְחָנֵּנוּ וְרַחֵם עָלֵינוּ, וְהוֹשִׁיעֵנוּ

כִּי אֵלֶיךָ עֵינֵינוּ, כִּי אֵל חַנּוּן וְרַחוּם אָתָּה.

וּבְנֵה יְרוּשָׁלַיִם עִיר הַקֹּדֶשׁ בִּמְהֵרָה בְיָמֵינוּ.

בָּרוּךְ אַתָּה יהוה, בּוֹנֵה בְרַחֲמָיו יְרוּשָׁלָיִם, אָמֵן.

BLESSED are You, LORD our God, King of the Universe –
God our Father, our King, our Sovereign,
our Creator, our Redeemer, our Maker,
our Holy One, the Holy One of Jacob.
He is our Shepherd, Israel's Shepherd,
the good King who does good to all.
Every day He has done, is doing, and will do good to us.
He has acted, is acting, and will always act kindly toward us for ever,
granting us grace, kindness and compassion, relief and rescue,
prosperity, blessing, redemption and comfort,
sustenance and support, compassion,
life, peace and all good things,
and of all good things may He never let us lack.

MAY THE COMPASSIONATE ONE
reign over us for ever and all time.

MAY THE COMPASSIONATE ONE
be blessed in heaven and on the earth.

MAY THE COMPASSIONATE ONE
be praised from generation to generation,
be glorified by us to all eternity,
and honored among us for ever and all time.

MAY THE COMPASSIONATE ONE
grant us an honorable livelihood.

MAY THE COMPASSIONATE ONE
break the yoke from our neck
and lead us upstanding to our own land.

MAY THE COMPASSIONATE ONE
send us many blessings to this house
and this table at which we have eaten.

MAY THE COMPASSIONATE ONE
send us Elijah the prophet –
may he be remembered for good –
to bring us good tidings of salvation and consolation.

MAY THE COMPASSIONATE ONE
bless the state of Israel,
first flowering of our redemption.

בָּרוּךְ אַתָּה יהוה אֱלֹהֵינוּ מֶלֶךְ הָעוֹלָם
הָאֵל אָבִינוּ, מַלְכֵּנוּ, אַדִּירֵנוּ
בּוֹרְאֵנוּ, גּוֹאֲלֵנוּ, יוֹצְרֵנוּ, קְדוֹשֵׁנוּ, קְדוֹשׁ יַעֲקֹב
רוֹעֵנוּ, רוֹעֵה יִשְׂרָאֵל, הַמֶּלֶךְ הַטּוֹב וְהַמֵּיטִיב לַכֹּל, שֶׁבְּכָל יוֹם וָיוֹם
הוּא הֵיטִיב, הוּא מֵיטִיב, הוּא יֵיטִיב לָנוּ
הוּא גְמָלָנוּ, הוּא גוֹמְלֵנוּ, הוּא יִגְמְלֵנוּ לָעַד
לְחֵן וּלְחֶסֶד וּלְרַחֲמִים, וּלְרֶוַח, הַצָּלָה וְהַצְלָחָה
בְּרָכָה וִישׁוּעָה, נֶחָמָה, פַּרְנָסָה וְכַלְכָּלָה
וְרַחֲמִים וְחַיִּים וְשָׁלוֹם וְכָל טוֹב, וּמִכָּל טוּב לְעוֹלָם אַל יְחַסְּרֵנוּ.

הָרַחֲמָן הוּא יִמְלֹךְ עָלֵינוּ לְעוֹלָם וָעֶד.

הָרַחֲמָן הוּא יִתְבָּרַךְ בַּשָּׁמַיִם וּבָאָרֶץ.

הָרַחֲמָן הוּא יִשְׁתַּבַּח לְדוֹר דּוֹרִים
וְיִתְפָּאַר בָּנוּ לָעַד וּלְנֵצַח נְצָחִים
וְיִתְהַדַּר בָּנוּ לָעַד וּלְעוֹלְמֵי עוֹלָמִים.

הָרַחֲמָן הוּא יְפַרְנְסֵנוּ בְּכָבוֹד.

הָרַחֲמָן הוּא יִשְׁבֹּר עֻלֵּנוּ מֵעַל צַוָּארֵנוּ
וְהוּא יוֹלִיכֵנוּ קוֹמְמִיּוּת לְאַרְצֵנוּ.

הָרַחֲמָן הוּא יִשְׁלַח לָנוּ
בְּרָכָה מְרֻבָּה בַּבַּיִת הַזֶּה
וְעַל שֻׁלְחָן זֶה שֶׁאָכַלְנוּ עָלָיו.

הָרַחֲמָן הוּא יִשְׁלַח לָנוּ
אֶת אֵלִיָּהוּ הַנָּבִיא זָכוּר לַטּוֹב
וִיבַשֶּׂר לָנוּ בְּשׂוֹרוֹת טוֹבוֹת יְשׁוּעוֹת וְנֶחָמוֹת.

הָרַחֲמָן הוּא יְבָרֵךְ
אֶת מְדִינַת יִשְׂרָאֵל
רֵאשִׁית צְמִיחַת גְּאֻלָּתֵנוּ.

MAY THE COMPASSIONATE ONE
  bless the members of Israel's Defense Forces,
  who stand guard over our land.

When eating at one's own table, say (include the words in parentheses that apply):

MAY THE COMPASSIONATE ONE bless –
  me, (my wife/my husband/my father, my teacher/
  my mother, my teacher/my children,) and all that is mine,

  A guest at someone else's table says (include the words in parentheses that apply):
  the master of this house, him (and his wife, the mistress of this house/
  and his children) and all that is his,

  Children at their parents' table say (include the words in parentheses that apply):
  my father, my teacher (master of this house), and my mother,
  my teacher (mistress of this house), them, their household, their
  children, and all that is theirs.

  For all other guests, add:
  and all the diners here,

together with us and all that is ours.
Just as our forefathers
Abraham, Isaac and Jacob were blessed in all, from all, with all,
so may He bless all of us together with a complete blessing,
and let us say: Amen.

ON HIGH, may grace be invoked for them and for us,
as a safeguard of peace.
May we receive a blessing from the LORD
and a just reward from the God of our salvation,
and may we find grace and good favor in the eyes of God and man.

On Shabbat: **MAY THE COMPASSIONATE ONE**   let us inherit the time, that will be entirely
                                                Shabbat and rest for life everlasting

MAY THE COMPASSIONATE ONE   let us inherit the day, that is all good.

MAY THE COMPASSIONATE ONE   make us worthy of the Messianic Age and life in the
                                  World to Come.

He is a tower of salvation to His king,
showing kindness to His anointed,
to David and his descendants for ever.
He who makes peace in His high places,
may He make peace for us and all Israel,
and let us say: Amen

הָרַחֲמָן הוּא יְבָרֵךְ
אֶת חַיָּלֵי צְבָא הַהֲגָנָה לְיִשְׂרָאֵל
הָעוֹמְדִים עַל מִשְׁמַר אַרְצֵנוּ.

בעל הבית ובעלת הבית אומרים:

הָרַחֲמָן הוּא יְבָרֵךְ אוֹתִי,
(וְאֶת אִשְׁתִּי / וְאֶת בַּעֲלִי / וְאֶת אָבִי מוֹרִי / וְאֶת אִמִּי מוֹרָתִי / וְאֶת זַרְעִי)
וְאֶת כָּל אֲשֶׁר לִי

ילדים האוכלים על שולחן הוריהם אומרים:

הָרַחֲמָן הוּא יְבָרֵךְ אֶת אָבִי מוֹרִי, (בַּעַל הַבַּיִת הַזֶּה)
וְאֶת אִמִּי מוֹרָתִי, (בַּעֲלַת הַבַּיִת הַזֶּה)
אוֹתָם וְאֶת בֵּיתָם וְאֶת זַרְעָם וְאֶת כָּל אֲשֶׁר לָהֶם

אורח אומר:

הָרַחֲמָן הוּא יְבָרֵךְ אֶת בַּעַל הַבַּיִת הַזֶּה, וְאֶת בַּעֲלַת הַבַּיִת הַזֶּה
אוֹתָם וְאֶת בֵּיתָם וְאֶת זַרְעָם וְאֶת כָּל אֲשֶׁר לָהֶם

אם יש אורחים נוספים, מוסיפים:

וְאֶת כָּל הַמְּסֻבִּין כָּאן
אוֹתָם וְאֶת בֵּיתָם וְאֶת זַרְעָם וְאֶת כָּל אֲשֶׁר לָהֶם

אוֹתָנוּ וְאֶת כָּל אֲשֶׁר לָנוּ כְּמוֹ שֶׁנִּתְבָּרְכוּ אֲבוֹתֵינוּ
אַבְרָהָם יִצְחָק וְיַעֲקֹב, בַּכֹּל, מִכֹּל, כֹּל
כֵּן יְבָרֵךְ אוֹתָנוּ כֻּלָּנוּ יַחַד בִּבְרָכָה שְׁלֵמָה,
וְנֹאמַר אָמֵן.

בַּמָּרוֹם יְלַמְּדוּ עֲלֵיהֶם וְעָלֵינוּ זְכוּת שֶׁתְּהֵא לְמִשְׁמֶרֶת שָׁלוֹם
_ז_ וְנִשָּׂא בְרָכָה מֵאֵת יְהוה וּצְדָקָה מֵאֱלֹהֵי יִשְׁעֵנוּ
וְנִמְצָא חֵן וְשֵׂכֶל טוֹב בְּעֵינֵי אֱלֹהִים וְאָדָם.

בשבת: הָרַחֲמָן הוּא יַנְחִילֵנוּ יוֹם שֶׁכֻּלּוֹ שַׁבָּת
וּמְנוּחָה לְחַיֵּי הָעוֹלָמִים.

הָרַחֲמָן הוּא יַנְחִילֵנוּ יוֹם שֶׁכֻּלּוֹ טוֹב.

הָרַחֲמָן הוּא יְזַכֵּנוּ לִימוֹת הַמָּשִׁיחַ וּלְחַיֵּי הָעוֹלָם הַבָּא
מִגְדּוֹל יְשׁוּעוֹת מַלְכּוֹ וְעֹשֶׂה-חֶסֶד לִמְשִׁיחוֹ לְדָוִד וּלְזַרְעוֹ עַד-עוֹלָם:
עֹשֶׂה שָׁלוֹם בִּמְרוֹמָיו הוּא יַעֲשֶׂה שָׁלוֹם עָלֵינוּ וְעַל כָּל יִשְׂרָאֵל וְאִמְרוּ אָמֵן.

יְראוּ אֶת־יהוה קְדֹשָׁיו כִּי־אֵין מַחְסוֹר לִירֵאָיו:
כְּפִירִים רָשׁוּ וְרָעֵבוּ וְדֹרְשֵׁי יהוה לֹא־יַחְסְרוּ כָל־טוֹב:
הוֹדוּ לַיהוה כִּי־טוֹב כִּי לְעוֹלָם חַסְדּוֹ:
פּוֹתֵחַ אֶת־יָדֶךָ וּמַשְׂבִּיעַ לְכָל־חַי רָצוֹן:
בָּרוּךְ הַגֶּבֶר אֲשֶׁר יִבְטַח בַּיהוה וְהָיָה יהוה מִבְטַחוֹ:
נַעַר הָיִיתִי גַּם־זָקַנְתִּי וְלֹא־רָאִיתִי צַדִּיק נֶעֱזָב וְזַרְעוֹ מְבַקֶּשׁ־לָחֶם:
יהוה עֹז לְעַמּוֹ יִתֵּן יהוה יְבָרֵךְ אֶת־עַמּוֹ בַשָּׁלוֹם:

הִנְנִי מוּכָן וּמְזוּמָן לְקַיֵּים מִצְוַות כּוֹס שְׁלִישִׁי שֶׁל אַרְבַּע כּוֹסוֹת.
לְשֵׁם יִחוּד קוּדְשָׁא בְּרִיךְ הוּא וּשְׁכִינְתֵּיהּ עַל יְדֵי הַהוּא טָמִיר וְנֶעֱלָם בְּשֵׁם כָּל יִשְׂרָאֵל.

בָּרוּךְ אַתָּה יהוה אֱלֹהֵינוּ מֶלֶךְ הָעוֹלָם
בּוֹרֵא פְּרִי הַגָּפֶן.

שׁוֹתִים כּוֹס שְׁלִישִׁי בַּהֲסִבַּת שְׂמֹאל.

FEAR the LORD, you His holy ones;
those who fear Him lack nothing.
Young lions may grow weak and hungry,
but those who seek the LORD lack no good thing.
Thank the LORD for He is good: His loving-kindness is for ever.
You open Your hand and satisfy the desire of every living thing.
Blessed is the person who trusts in the LORD, whose trust is in the LORD alone.
Once I was young, and now I am old,
yet I have never watched a righteous man forsaken or his children begging for bread.
The LORD will give His people strength.
The LORD will bless His people with peace.

I am hereby prepared and ready to fulfill the commandment of the third of the four cups.
For the sake of the unification of the Holy One, blessed be He, and His Divine Presence,
through that which is hidden and concealed, in the name of all Israel.

Blessed are You, LORD our God, King of the Universe,
who creates fruit of the vine.

Drink while reclining to the left.

GRACE AFTER MEALS

May the Lord God of Israel be blessed
The Lord our God who is blessed,

Every day,
Every year,
Every month,
Every hour of every day,

Every last moment,
In His goodness and entirety,
    the Lord renews His name.

May His name be blessed
Now and forever.

As we ate our fill
And, having drunk and enjoyed,

We now bless the Lord our God,
And recall the Lord now
Lest we forget […]

(*Identity and Tradition*, 68)

Healing prayer amulet

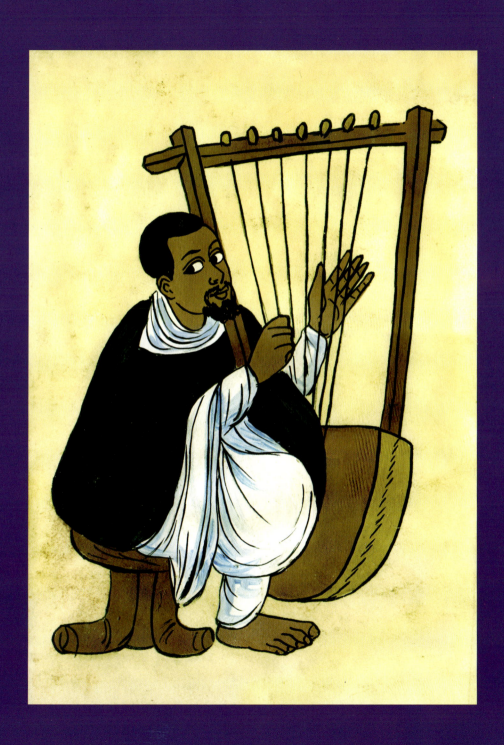

שְׁפֹךְ חֲמָתְךָ אֶל־הַגּוֹיִם
אֲשֶׁר לֹא־יְדָעוּךָ
וְעַל מַמְלָכוֹת
אֲשֶׁר בְּשִׁמְךָ לֹא קָרָאוּ:
כִּי אָכַל אֶת־יַעֲקֹב
וְאֶת־נָוֵהוּ הֵשַׁמּוּ:

שְׁפָךְ־עֲלֵיהֶם זַעְמֶךָ
וַחֲרוֹן אַפְּךָ יַשִּׂיגֵם:
תִּרְדֹּף בְּאַף וְתַשְׁמִידֵם
מִתַּחַת שְׁמֵי יהוה:

A cup of wine is now poured in honor of Eliyahu, and the door is opened.

POUR OUT

Your wrath upon the nations that do not know You,
and on the kingdoms that do not call on Your name.
For they have devoured Jacob
and laid waste his dwelling place.
Pour out Your indignation upon them,
and let Your fierce anger overtake them.
Pursue them with wrath and destroy them,
from beneath the heavens of the LORD.

The door is closed.

153

HALLEL

The fourth cup of wine is poured, and Hallel is completed.

Not to us, Lord, not to us,
but to Your name give glory,
for Your love, for Your faithfulness.
Why should the nations say, "Where now is their God?"
Our God is in heaven; whatever He wills He does.
Their idols are silver and gold, made by human hands.
They have mouths but cannot speak;
eyes but cannot see.
They have ears but cannot hear;
noses but cannot smell.
They have hands but cannot feel;
feet but cannot walk.
No sound comes from their throat.
Those who make them become like them;
so will all who trust in them.
Israel, trust in the Lord –
He is their Help and Shield.
House of Aaron, trust in the Lord –
He is their Help and their Shield.
You who fear the Lord, trust in the Lord –
He is their Help and Shield.

The Lord remembers us and will bless us.
He will bless the house of Israel. He will bless the house of Aaron.
He will bless those who fear the Lord, small and great alike.
May the Lord give you increase: you and your children.
May you be blessed by the Lord, Maker of heaven and earth.
The heavens are the Lord's, but the earth He has given over to mankind.
It is not the dead who praise the Lord,
nor those who go down to the silent grave.
But we will bless the Lord, now and for ever.

HALLELUYA!

מוזגים כוס רביעי וגומרים עליו את ההלל:

לֹא לָנוּ יהוה לֹא לָנוּ

כִּי־לְשִׁמְךָ תֵּן כָּבוֹד

עַל־חַסְדְּךָ עַל־אֲמִתֶּךָ:

לָמָּה יֹאמְרוּ הַגּוֹיִם אַיֵּה־נָא אֱלֹהֵיהֶם:

וֵאלֹהֵינוּ בַשָּׁמָיִם, כֹּל אֲשֶׁר־חָפֵץ עָשָׂה:

עֲצַבֵּיהֶם כֶּסֶף וְזָהָב, מַעֲשֵׂה יְדֵי אָדָם:

פֶּה־לָהֶם וְלֹא יְדַבֵּרוּ, עֵינַיִם לָהֶם וְלֹא יִרְאוּ:

אָזְנַיִם לָהֶם וְלֹא יִשְׁמָעוּ, אַף לָהֶם וְלֹא יְרִיחוּן:

יְדֵיהֶם וְלֹא יְמִישׁוּן, רַגְלֵיהֶם וְלֹא יְהַלֵּכוּ, לֹא־יֶהְגּוּ בִּגְרוֹנָם:

כְּמוֹהֶם יִהְיוּ עֹשֵׂיהֶם, כֹּל אֲשֶׁר־בֹּטֵחַ בָּהֶם:

יִשְׂרָאֵל בְּטַח בַּיהוה, עֶזְרָם וּמָגִנָּם הוּא:

בֵּית אַהֲרֹן בִּטְחוּ בַיהוה, עֶזְרָם וּמָגִנָּם הוּא:

יִרְאֵי יהוה בִּטְחוּ בַיהוה, עֶזְרָם וּמָגִנָּם הוּא:

יהוה זְכָרָנוּ יְבָרֵךְ

יְבָרֵךְ אֶת־בֵּית יִשְׂרָאֵל, יְבָרֵךְ אֶת־בֵּית אַהֲרֹן:

יְבָרֵךְ יִרְאֵי יהוה, הַקְּטַנִּים עִם־הַגְּדֹלִים:

יֹסֵף יהוה עֲלֵיכֶם, עֲלֵיכֶם וְעַל־בְּנֵיכֶם:

בְּרוּכִים אַתֶּם לַיהוה, עֹשֵׂה שָׁמַיִם וָאָרֶץ:

הַשָּׁמַיִם שָׁמַיִם לַיהוה, וְהָאָרֶץ נָתַן לִבְנֵי־אָדָם:

לֹא הַמֵּתִים יְהַלְלוּ־יָהּ, וְלֹא כָּל־יֹרְדֵי דוּמָה:

וַאֲנַחְנוּ נְבָרֵךְ יָהּ, מֵעַתָּה וְעַד־עוֹלָם

הַלְלוּיָהּ:

I love the Lord who hears my voice and my supplications.
Because He has inclined His ear to me,
therefore I will call upon Him as long as I live.
The cords of death surrounded me,
and the pains of She'ol seized upon me:
I found trouble and sorrow.
Then I called upon the name of the Lord;
O Lord, I beseech You, deliver my soul.
Gracious is the Lord, and just; and our God is merciful.
The Lord preserves the simple:
I was brought low, and He saved me.
Return to your rest, O my soul;
for the Lord has dealt bountifully with you.
For You have delivered my soul from death,
my eyes from tears, and my feet from falling.
I will walk before the Lord in the land of the living.
I kept faith even when I said, I am greatly afflicted.
I said in my haste, every man is false.

How can I repay the Lord for all His benefits toward me?
I will raise the cup of salvation and call upon the name of the Lord.
I will pay my vows to the Lord now in the presence of all His people.
Precious in the sight of the Lord is the death of His pious ones.
O Lord, truly I am Your servant;
I am Your servant, the son of Your handmaid:
You have loosed my bonds.
I will offer to you the sacrifice of thanksgiving,
and I will call upon the name of the Lord.
I will pay my vows to the Lord
in the presence of all His people,
In the courts of the Lord's house,
in your midst, Jerusalem.

HALLELUYA!

אָהַבְתִּי, כִּי־יִשְׁמַע יהוה, אֶת־קוֹלִי תַּחֲנוּנָי:

כִּי־הִטָּה אָזְנוֹ לִי, וּבְיָמַי אֶקְרָא:

אֲפָפוּנִי חֶבְלֵי־מָוֶת, וּמְצָרֵי שְׁאוֹל מְצָאוּנִי, צָרָה וְיָגוֹן אֶמְצָא:

וּבְשֵׁם־יהוה אֶקְרָא, אָנָּה יהוה מַלְּטָה נַפְשִׁי:

חַנּוּן יהוה וְצַדִּיק, וֵאלֹהֵינוּ מְרַחֵם:

שֹׁמֵר פְּתָאיִם יהוה, דַּלּוֹתִי וְלִי יְהוֹשִׁיעַ:

שׁוּבִי נַפְשִׁי לִמְנוּחָיְכִי, כִּי־יהוה גָּמַל עָלָיְכִי:

כִּי חִלַּצְתָּ נַפְשִׁי מִמָּוֶת

אֶת־עֵינִי מִן־דִּמְעָה

אֶת־רַגְלִי מִדֶּחִי:

אֶתְהַלֵּךְ לִפְנֵי יהוה, בְּאַרְצוֹת הַחַיִּים:

הֶאֱמַנְתִּי כִּי אֲדַבֵּר, אֲנִי עָנִיתִי מְאֹד:

אֲנִי אָמַרְתִּי בְחָפְזִי, כָּל־הָאָדָם כֹּזֵב:

מָה־אָשִׁיב לַיהוה, כָּל־תַּגְמוּלוֹהִי עָלָי:

כּוֹס־יְשׁוּעוֹת אֶשָּׂא, וּבְשֵׁם יהוה אֶקְרָא:

נְדָרַי לַיהוה אֲשַׁלֵּם, נֶגְדָה־נָּא לְכָל־עַמּוֹ:

יָקָר בְּעֵינֵי יהוה, הַמָּוְתָה לַחֲסִידָיו:

אָנָּה יהוה כִּי־אֲנִי עַבְדֶּךָ

אֲנִי־עַבְדְּךָ בֶּן־אֲמָתֶךָ, פִּתַּחְתָּ לְמוֹסֵרָי:

לְךָ־אֶזְבַּח זֶבַח תּוֹדָה, וּבְשֵׁם יהוה אֶקְרָא:

נְדָרַי לַיהוה אֲשַׁלֵּם, נֶגְדָה־נָּא לְכָל־עַמּוֹ:

בְּחַצְרוֹת בֵּית יהוה, בְּתוֹכֵכִי יְרוּשָׁלָ‍ִם

הַלְלוּיָהּ:

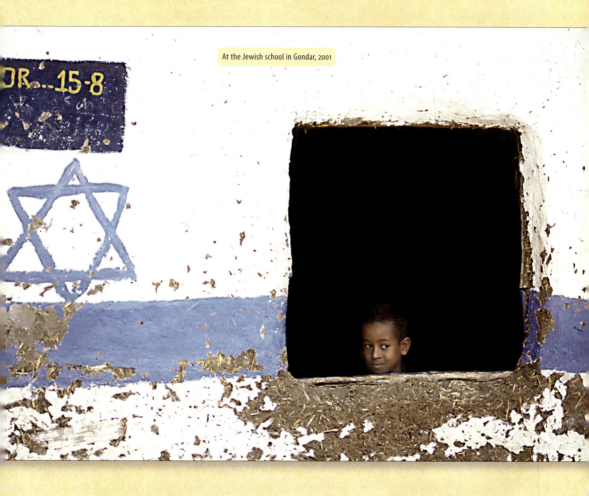

At the Jewish school in Gondar, 2001

הַלְלוּ

אֶת־יהוה כָּל־גּוֹיִם, שַׁבְּחוּהוּ כָּל־הָאֻמִּים:
כִּי גָבַר עָלֵינוּ חַסְדּוֹ, וֶאֱמֶת־יהוה לְעוֹלָם

הַלְלוּיָהּ:

כִּי לְעוֹלָם חַסְדּוֹ:	הוֹדוּ לַיהוה כִּי־טוֹב
כִּי לְעוֹלָם חַסְדּוֹ:	יֹאמַר־נָא יִשְׂרָאֵל
כִּי לְעוֹלָם חַסְדּוֹ:	יֹאמְרוּ־נָא בֵית־אַהֲרֹן
כִּי לְעוֹלָם חַסְדּוֹ:	יֹאמְרוּ־נָא יִרְאֵי יהוה

O PRAISE

the LORD, all you nations:
praise Him, all you peoples.
For His love for us is great:
and the truth of the LORD endures forever.

HALLELUYA!

O give thanks to the LORD; for He is good:
FOR HIS STEADFAST LOVE ENDURES FOREVER.

Let Israel now say,
THAT HIS STEADFAST LOVE ENDURES FOREVER.

Let the house of Aaron now say,
THAT HIS STEADFAST LOVE ENDURES FOREVER.

Let those now who fear the LORD say,
THAT HIS STEADFAST LOVE ENDURES FOREVER.

Out of my distress I called upon the LORD:
the LORD answered me with liberation.
The LORD is on my side; I will not fear: what can a man do to me?
The LORD takes my part with those who help me:
therefore shall I gaze upon those who hate me.
It is better to take refuge in the LORD than to put confidence in man.
It is better to take refuge in the LORD than to trust in princes.
All nations compassed me about:
but in the name of the LORD I cut them off.
They compassed me about; indeed they surrounded me:
but in the name of the LORD I cut them off.
They compassed me about like bees;
they are quenched like a fire of thorns;
for in the name of the LORD I cut them off.
You did push me hard that I might fall: but the LORD helped me.
The LORD is my strength and song, and is become my salvation.
The voice of rejoicing and salvation is in the tents of the righteous:
the right hand of the LORD does valiantly.
The right hand of the LORD is exalted:
the right hand of the LORD does valiantly.
I shall not die, but live and declare the works of the LORD.
The LORD has chastised me severely:
but He has not given me up to death.
Open to me the gates of righteousness:
I will go into them, and I will praise the LORD:
This is the gate of the LORD: into which the righteous shall enter.

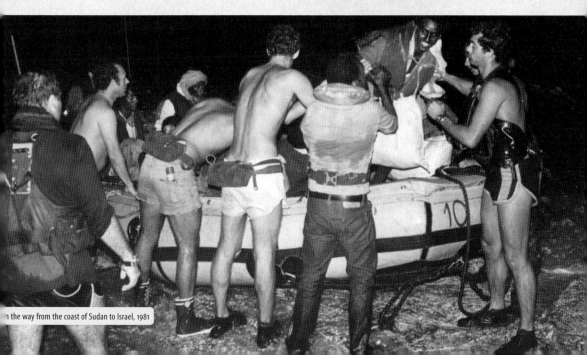

n the way from the coast of Sudan to Israel, 1981

Gondar, 2001

מִן־הַמֵּצַר קָרָאתִי יָּהּ,

עָנָנִי בַמֶּרְחָב יָהּ:

יהוה לִי לֹא אִירָא,

מַה־יַּעֲשֶׂה לִי אָדָם:

יהוה לִי בְּעֹזְרָי,

וַאֲנִי אֶרְאֶה בְשֹׂנְאָי:

טוֹב לַחֲסוֹת בַּיהוה,

מִבְּטֹחַ בָּאָדָם:

טוֹב לַחֲסוֹת בַּיהוה,

מִבְּטֹחַ בִּנְדִיבִים:

כָּל־גּוֹיִם סְבָבוּנִי,

בְּשֵׁם יהוה כִּי אֲמִילַם:

סַבּוּנִי גַם־סְבָבוּנִי,

בְּשֵׁם יהוה כִּי אֲמִילַם:

סַבּוּנִי כִדְבֹרִים,

דֹּעֲכוּ כְּאֵשׁ קוֹצִים

בְּשֵׁם יהוה כִּי אֲמִילַם:

דָּחֹה דְחִיתַנִי לִנְפֹּל, וַיהוה עֲזָרָנִי:

עָזִּי וְזִמְרָת יָהּ, וַיְהִי־לִי לִישׁוּעָה:

קוֹל רִנָּה וִישׁוּעָה בְּאָהֳלֵי צַדִּיקִים,

יְמִין יהוה עֹשָׂה חָיִל:

יְמִין יהוה רוֹמֵמָה, יְמִין יהוה עֹשָׂה חָיִל:

לֹא־אָמוּת כִּי־אֶחְיֶה, וַאֲסַפֵּר מַעֲשֵׂי יָהּ:

יַסֹּר יִסְּרַנִּי יָּהּ, וְלַמָּוֶת לֹא נְתָנָנִי:

פִּתְחוּ־לִי שַׁעֲרֵי־צֶדֶק, אָבֹא־בָם אוֹדֶה יָהּ:

זֶה־הַשַּׁעַר לַיהוה, צַדִּיקִים יָבֹאוּ בוֹ:

I will give thanks to You, for You have answered me,
and have become my salvation.

I WILL GIVE THANKS TO YOU, FOR YOU HAVE ANSWERED ME,
AND HAVE BECOME MY SALVATION.

The stone which the builders rejected
has become the headstone of the corner.

THE STONE WHICH THE BUILDERS REJECTED
HAS BECOME THE HEADSTONE OF THE CORNER.

This is the Lord's doing; it is marvellous in our eyes.

THIS IS THE LORD'S DOING; IT IS MARVELLOUS IN OUR EYES.

This is the day which the Lord has made; we will rejoice and be glad in it.

THIS IS THE DAY WHICH THE LORD HAS MADE;
WE WILL REJOICE AND BE GLAD IN IT.

SAVE US, O LORD, WE PRAY YOU

SAVE US, O LORD, WE PRAY YOU

WE PRAY YOU, O LORD, PROSPER US

WE PRAY YOU, O LORD, PROSPER US

Blessed is he who comes in the name of the Lord:
we have blessed you out of the house of the Lord.

BLESSED IS HE WHO COMES IN THE NAME OF THE LORD:
WE HAVE BLESSED YOU OUT OF THE HOUSE OF THE LORD.

God is the Lord, who has shown us light:
bind the sacrifice with cords, to the horns of the altar.

GOD IS THE LORD, WHO HAS SHOWN US LIGHT:
BIND THE SACRIFICE WITH CORDS, TO THE HORNS OF THE ALTAR.

You are my God, and I will praise You: my God, I will exalt You.

YOU ARE MY GOD, AND I WILL PRAISE YOU: MY GOD, I WILL EXALT YOU.

O give thanks to the Lord; for He is good:
for His steadfast love endures forever.

O GIVE THANKS TO THE LORD; FOR HE IS GOOD:
FOR HIS STEADFAST LOVE ENDURES FOREVER.

אוֹדְךָ כִּי עֲנִיתָנִי, וַתְּהִי־לִי לִישׁוּעָה:

אוֹדְךָ כִּי עֲנִיתָנִי, וַתְּהִי־לִי לִישׁוּעָה:

אֶבֶן מָאֲסוּ הַבּוֹנִים, הָיְתָה לְרֹאשׁ פִּנָּה:

אֶבֶן מָאֲסוּ הַבּוֹנִים, הָיְתָה לְרֹאשׁ פִּנָּה:

מֵאֵת יהוה הָיְתָה זֹּאת, הִיא נִפְלָאת בְּעֵינֵינוּ:

מֵאֵת יהוה הָיְתָה זֹּאת, הִיא נִפְלָאת בְּעֵינֵינוּ:

זֶה־הַיּוֹם עָשָׂה יהוה, נָגִילָה וְנִשְׂמְחָה בוֹ:

זֶה־הַיּוֹם עָשָׂה יהוה, נָגִילָה וְנִשְׂמְחָה בוֹ:

אָנָּא יהוה הוֹשִׁיעָה נָּא:

אָנָּא יהוה הוֹשִׁיעָה נָּא:

אָנָּא יהוה הַצְלִיחָה נָא:

אָנָּא יהוה הַצְלִיחָה נָא:

בָּרוּךְ הַבָּא בְּשֵׁם יהוה, בֵּרַכְנוּכֶם מִבֵּית יהוה:

בָּרוּךְ הַבָּא בְּשֵׁם יהוה, בֵּרַכְנוּכֶם מִבֵּית יהוה:

אֵל יהוה וַיָּאֶר לָנוּ, אִסְרוּ־חַג בַּעֲבֹתִים עַד־קַרְנוֹת הַמִּזְבֵּחַ:

אֵל יהוה וַיָּאֶר לָנוּ, אִסְרוּ־חַג בַּעֲבֹתִים עַד־קַרְנוֹת הַמִּזְבֵּחַ:

אֵלִי אַתָּה וְאוֹדֶךָּ, אֱלֹהַי אֲרוֹמְמֶךָּ:

אֵלִי אַתָּה וְאוֹדֶךָּ, אֱלֹהַי אֲרוֹמְמֶךָּ:

הוֹדוּ לַיהוה כִּי־טוֹב, כִּי לְעוֹלָם חַסְדּוֹ:

הוֹדוּ לַיהוה כִּי־טוֹב, כִּי לְעוֹלָם חַסְדּוֹ:

יְהַלְלוּךָ

יהוה אֱלֹהֵינוּ כָּל מַעֲשֶׂיךָ

וַחֲסִידֶיךָ צַדִּיקִים עוֹשֵׂי רְצוֹנֶךָ

וְכָל עַמְּךָ בֵּית יִשְׂרָאֵל

בְּרִנָּה יוֹדוּ וִיבָרְכוּ וִישַׁבְּחוּ

וִיפָאֲרוּ וִירוֹמְמוּ וְיַעֲרִיצוּ

וְיַקְדִּישׁוּ וְיַמְלִיכוּ אֶת שִׁמְךָ מַלְכֵּנוּ

כִּי לְךָ טוֹב לְהוֹדוֹת וּלְשִׁמְךָ נָאֶה לְזַמֵּר

כִּי מֵעוֹלָם וְעַד עוֹלָם

אַתָּה אֵל.

May all Your creatures

PRAISE YOU;

together with Your pious and righteous ones who do Your will,
and may all Your people, the house of Israel,
give joyful thanks, and bless, and honor,
and glorify, and exalt, and reverence,
and sanctify, and esteem with royal tribute,
Your name, our King.
For to You it is good to give thanks,
and to Your name it is fitting to sing a melody,
for from everlasting to everlasting

YOU ARE GOD.

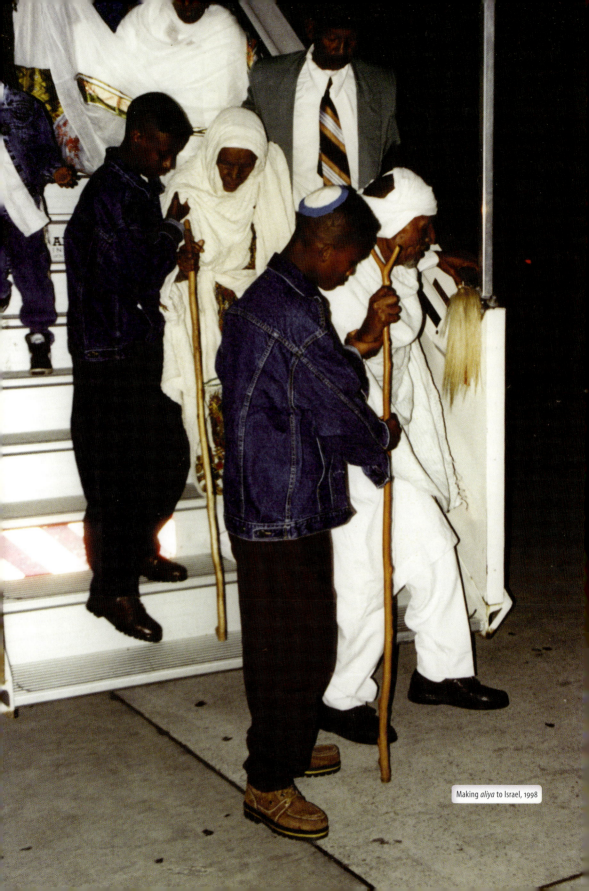

Making *aliya* to Israel, 1998

HALLELUYA, PRAISE SUITS YOU, O LORD

Halleluya, praise suits You,
Dear Lord, in Your honor and grandeur.
    O lofty One
Enthroned upon Your seat on high,
    for You are the glory
of the righteous, the crown of the pure,
    the grandeur of the
humble and the strength of the weak.

Halleluya to the One Lord, holy,
holy, holy. For You are compassionate
    and forgiving.
You raise up the lowly and lay low
the haughty. You alone are King and Master
of justice and loving-kindness.

Praise to the Lord, the One and only,
    O lofty One residing
in the heavens. Blessed be He unto His
    great heavenly heights,
For His name is holy and pure.
    Give praise and honor
to the Lord of heaven and earth.

Praise to the praiseworthy Lord,
    Who has guarded me,
rescued me and showed me compassion
    since my youth whenever I suffered
from famine, or pestilence, or war,
    or disease.
When my feet faltered and I fell into pits or
    high water.

When I fell prey to the beasts of the field or
    fierce birds
in the skies; those birds who ate their
flesh, while the beasts of the field drank
    their blood; the Lord gave me strength,
Although He knew of all my sinful ways
And understood the impurity in my heart.
For the Lord is righteous, compassionate,
    slow to anger,
And full of pity and loving-kindness.
    The compassionate, forgiving One
Restrained His anger in his love, kindness
and compassion; pious One, completely
    truthful One,
Who has protected me and brought me
    (to the heavens), just as
He does for all His righteous followers and
    attendant angels;
For the Lord's justice is not like our earthly
    justice.
Blessed and praised be the name of the
    blessed Lord God.

(Leslau)

BEFORE YOU THERE WAS NO OTHER GOD

You reside in the heavens on high,
And all the hosts of heaven shall sing Your
   praises.

Your throne is in the heavens on high, my
   Master,
And the entire universe is the work of Your
   hands.

Our eyes have not seen;
Our ears have not heard;
Our hearts have not felt,
And our minds have not imagined;

Any other Lord than You. Before You there was
No other God; and in Your wake – there is
   nothing without You.

O Lord who did create everything there is,
   You are God
alone, since time immemorial you have existed
   and forever after
You shall exist.

You are the first and the last, now and
forever after. For You are the Lord and
You shall never cease to be.

(Wurmbrand)

The nazirite Bayene Demoze, Wolleka, 1984

הוֹדוּ לַיהוה כִּי־טוֹב כִּי לְעוֹלָם חַסְדּוֹ:

הוֹדוּ לֵאלֹהֵי הָאֱלֹהִים כִּי לְעוֹלָם חַסְדּוֹ:

הוֹדוּ לַאֲדֹנֵי הָאֲדֹנִים כִּי לְעוֹלָם חַסְדּוֹ:

לְעֹשֵׂה נִפְלָאוֹת גְּדֹלוֹת לְבַדּוֹ כִּי לְעוֹלָם חַסְדּוֹ:

לְעֹשֵׂה הַשָּׁמַיִם בִּתְבוּנָה כִּי לְעוֹלָם חַסְדּוֹ:

לְרֹקַע הָאָרֶץ עַל־הַמָּיִם כִּי לְעוֹלָם חַסְדּוֹ:

לְעֹשֵׂה אוֹרִים גְּדֹלִים כִּי לְעוֹלָם חַסְדּוֹ:

אֶת־הַשֶּׁמֶשׁ לְמֶמְשֶׁלֶת בַּיּוֹם כִּי לְעוֹלָם חַסְדּוֹ:

אֶת־הַיָּרֵחַ וְכוֹכָבִים לְמֶמְשְׁלוֹת בַּלָּיְלָה כִּי לְעוֹלָם חַסְדּוֹ:

לְמַכֵּה מִצְרַיִם בִּבְכוֹרֵיהֶם כִּי לְעוֹלָם חַסְדּוֹ:

וַיּוֹצֵא יִשְׂרָאֵל מִתּוֹכָם כִּי לְעוֹלָם חַסְדּוֹ:

בְּיָד חֲזָקָה וּבִזְרוֹעַ נְטוּיָה כִּי לְעוֹלָם חַסְדּוֹ:

לְגֹזֵר יַם־סוּף לִגְזָרִים כִּי לְעוֹלָם חַסְדּוֹ:

וְהֶעֱבִיר יִשְׂרָאֵל בְּתוֹכוֹ כִּי לְעוֹלָם חַסְדּוֹ:

וְנִעֵר פַּרְעֹה וְחֵילוֹ בְיַם־סוּף כִּי לְעוֹלָם חַסְדּוֹ:

לְמוֹלִיךְ עַמּוֹ בַּמִּדְבָּר כִּי לְעוֹלָם חַסְדּוֹ:

לְמַכֵּה מְלָכִים גְּדֹלִים כִּי לְעוֹלָם חַסְדּוֹ:

וַיַּהֲרֹג מְלָכִים אַדִּירִים כִּי לְעוֹלָם חַסְדּוֹ:

לְסִיחוֹן מֶלֶךְ הָאֱמֹרִי כִּי לְעוֹלָם חַסְדּוֹ:

וּלְעוֹג מֶלֶךְ הַבָּשָׁן כִּי לְעוֹלָם חַסְדּוֹ:

וְנָתַן אַרְצָם לְנַחֲלָה כִּי לְעוֹלָם חַסְדּוֹ:

נַחֲלָה לְיִשְׂרָאֵל עַבְדּוֹ כִּי לְעוֹלָם חַסְדּוֹ:

שֶׁבְּשִׁפְלֵנוּ זָכַר לָנוּ כִּי לְעוֹלָם חַסְדּוֹ:

וַיִּפְרְקֵנוּ מִצָּרֵינוּ כִּי לְעוֹלָם חַסְדּוֹ:

נֹתֵן לֶחֶם לְכָל־בָּשָׂר כִּי לְעוֹלָם חַסְדּוֹ:

הוֹדוּ לְאֵל הַשָּׁמָיִם כִּי לְעוֹלָם חַסְדּוֹ:

Thank the Lord, for He is good,	His loving-kindness is for ever.
Thank the God of gods,	His loving-kindness is for ever.
Thank the Lord of lords,	His loving-kindness is for ever.
To the One who alone works great wonders,	His loving-kindness is for ever.
Who made the heavens with wisdom,	His loving-kindness is for ever.
Who spread the earth upon the waters,	His loving-kindness is for ever.
Who made the great lights,	His loving-kindness is for ever.
The sun to rule by day,	His loving-kindness is for ever.
The moon and the stars to rule by night;	His loving-kindness is for ever.
Who struck Egypt through their firstborn,	His loving-kindness is for ever.
And brought out Israel from their midst,	His loving-kindness is for ever.
With a strong hand and outstretched arm,	His loving-kindness is for ever.
Who split the Reed Sea into parts,	His loving-kindness is for ever.
And made Israel pass through it,	His loving-kindness is for ever.
Casting Pharaoh and his army into the Reed Sea;	
	His loving-kindness is for ever.
Who led His people through the wilderness;	His loving-kindness is for ever.
Who struck down great kings,	His loving-kindness is for ever.
And slew mighty kings,	His loving-kindness is for ever.
Sihon, king of the Amorites,	His loving-kindness is for ever.
And Og, king of Bashan,	His loving-kindness is for ever.
And gave their land as a heritage,	His loving-kindness is for ever.
A heritage for His servant Israel;	His loving-kindness is for ever.
Who remembered us in our lowly state,	His loving-kindness is for ever.
And rescued us from our tormentors,	His loving-kindness is for ever.
Who gives food to all flesh,	His loving-kindness is for ever.
Give thanks to the God of heaven.	His loving-kindness is for ever.

YOU ARE GOOD, DEAR LORD. AMEN, HALLELUYA

You are good, dear Lord. Amen, Halleluya.
You are the chosen One, dear Lord. Amen,
   Halleluya.
You are candid and honest, dear Lord.
   Amen, Halleluya.
You are compassionate, dear Lord. Amen,
   Halleluya.
You are forgiving, dear Lord. Amen,
   Halleluya.
You are pure, dear Lord. Amen, Halleluya.
There is no impurity or iniquity in You,
   dear Lord. Amen, Halleluya.
You are supremely worthy of praise, dear
   Lord. Amen, Halleluya.
You shall be glorified, dear Lord. Amen,
   Halleluya.
You are awesome, dear Lord. Amen,
   Halleluya.
You are mighty, dear Lord. Amen,
   Halleluya.

You are wise, dear Lord. Amen, Halleluya.
You are faithful, dear Lord. Amen,
   Halleluya.
You are the Giver of life, dear Lord. Amen,
   Halleluya.
You raise the downtrodden, dear Lord.
   Amen, Halleluya.
You are the King of kings, dear Lord. Amen,
   Halleluya.
You are the Judge of judges, dear Lord.
   Amen, Halleluya.
You are the highest of all officers, dear Lord.
   Amen, Halleluya.
You are the Lord of lords, dear God. Amen,
   Halleluya.
You are eternally praiseworthy. Amen.
We hereby bow before You and give thanks
   to Your eternally everlasting name. Amen.

(*Arde'et*, 52)

נִשְׁמַת

כָּל חַי תְּבָרֵךְ אֶת שִׁמְךָ, יהוה אֱלֹהֵינוּ
וְרוּחַ כָּל בָּשָׂר תְּפָאֵר וּתְרוֹמֵם זִכְרְךָ מַלְכֵּנוּ תָּמִיד.
מִן הָעוֹלָם וְעַד הָעוֹלָם אַתָּה אֵל
וּמִבַּלְעָדֶיךָ אֵין לָנוּ מֶלֶךְ גּוֹאֵל וּמוֹשִׁיעַ
פּוֹדֶה וּמַצִּיל וּמְפַרְנֵס וּמְרַחֵם
בְּכָל עֵת צָרָה וְצוּקָה אֵין לָנוּ מֶלֶךְ אֶלָּא אַתָּה.
אֱלֹהֵי הָרִאשׁוֹנִים וְהָאַחֲרוֹנִים, אֱלוֹהַּ כָּל בְּרִיּוֹת
אֲדוֹן כָּל תּוֹלָדוֹת, הַמְהֻלָּל בְּרֹב הַתִּשְׁבָּחוֹת
הַמְנַהֵג עוֹלָמוֹ בְּחֶסֶד וּבְרִיּוֹתָיו בְּרַחֲמִים.
וַיהוה לֹא יָנוּם וְלֹא יִישָׁן
הַמְעוֹרֵר יְשֵׁנִים וְהַמֵּקִיץ נִרְדָּמִים
וְהַמֵּשִׂיחַ אִלְּמִים וְהַמַּתִּיר אֲסוּרִים
וְהַסּוֹמֵךְ נוֹפְלִים וְהַזּוֹקֵף כְּפוּפִים.
לְךָ לְבַדְּךָ אֲנַחְנוּ מוֹדִים.

THE SOUL

of all that lives shall bless Your name,
Lord our God,
and the spirit of all flesh shall always glorify
and exalt Your remembrance, our King.
From eternity to eternity You are God.
Without You, we have no King, Redeemer or Savior,
who liberates, rescues, sustains
and shows compassion in every time of trouble and distress.
We have no King but You, God of the first and last,
God of all creatures, Master of all ages,
extolled by a multitude of praises,
who guides His world with loving-kindness
and His creatures with compassion.
the Lord neither slumbers nor sleeps.
He rouses the sleepers and wakens the slumberers.
He makes the dumb speak, sets the bound free,
supports the fallen, and raises those bowed down.
To You alone we give thanks.

If our mouth were filled with
song like the sea,
and our tongue with
overflowing joy like the
waves of the sea;
and if our lips could open
as wide as the firmament to
praise You,
and our eyes could shine
with devotion
like the sun and the moon;
and if we could spread out
our hands in worship
like the wings of eagles;
and if our feet could run as
swiftly to Your service
as the feet of hinds–

Community priest with instruments for accompanying prayers, Ambover, 1971

we would still not manage to give You due thanks,
O LORD our God, and God of our fathers, to bless Your name,
or to acknowledge the thousandth part
or even the millionth part of the benefits
which You have bestowed upon our fathers and upon us.
For You have redeemed us out of Egypt, O LORD our God,
and You have delivered us from the house of slaves.
In hunger You have nourished us,
and in plenty You have supported us.
From the sword You have saved us,
and from pestilence You have rescued us;
from foul and lingering diseases You have given us relief,
and ever till now has Your merciful care been our aid,
and Your steadfast love our unfailing stay.
Do not forsake us, O LORD our God, forever.

אִלּוּ פִינוּ מָלֵא שִׁירָה כַּיָּם

וּלְשׁוֹנֵנוּ רִנָּה כַּהֲמוֹן גַּלָּיו

וְשִׂפְתוֹתֵינוּ שֶׁבַח כְּמֶרְחֲבֵי רָקִיעַ

וְעֵינֵינוּ מְאִירוֹת כַּשֶּׁמֶשׁ וְכַיָּרֵחַ

וְיָדֵינוּ פְרוּשׂוֹת כְּנִשְׁרֵי שָׁמָיִם

וְרַגְלֵינוּ קַלּוֹת כָּאַיָּלוֹת

אֵין אֲנַחְנוּ מַסְפִּיקִים לְהוֹדוֹת לְךָ

יהוה אֱלֹהֵינוּ וֵאלֹהֵי אֲבוֹתֵינוּ

וּלְבָרֵךְ אֶת שְׁמֶךָ

עַל אַחַת מֵאֶלֶף אֶלֶף אַלְפֵי אֲלָפִים

וְרִבֵּי רְבָבוֹת פְּעָמִים הַטּוֹבוֹת

שֶׁעָשִׂיתָ עִם אֲבוֹתֵינוּ וְעִמָּנוּ.

מִמִּצְרַיִם גְּאַלְתָּנוּ, יהוה אֱלֹהֵינוּ, וּמִבֵּית עֲבָדִים פְּדִיתָנוּ

בְּרָעָב זַנְתָּנוּ וּבְשָׂבָע כִּלְכַּלְתָּנוּ

מֵחֶרֶב הִצַּלְתָּנוּ וּמִדֶּבֶר מִלַּטְתָּנוּ

וּמֵחֳלָיִים רָעִים וְנֶאֱמָנִים דִּלִּיתָנוּ.

עַד הֵנָּה עֲזָרוּנוּ רַחֲמֶיךָ, וְלֹא עֲזָבוּנוּ חֲסָדֶיךָ

Prayers offered by the community priests for the Passover holiday, Uzava, 1963

173

In recognition of this, those limbs which You have granted us,
and the spirit which You have breathed into our nostrils,
and the tongue which You have set in our mouths,
will all join in praising, blessing,
acclaiming, glorifying,
adoring, exalting, revering, and hallowing
Your name, our King.
For to You every mouth shall give thanks;
and to You every tongue shall swear;
and to You every knee shall bow;
before You every upright form shall prostrate itself;
and all hearts shall fear You.
All bodies and organs shall sing to Your name,
according to the word that is written:
All my bones shall say, LORD, who is like You,
who delivers the poor man
from him that is too strong for him,
and the poor and the needy
from him that would rob him?
Who is like You? Who is equal to You?
Who may be compared to You?
A great, mighty, and terrible God,
God supreme, Owner of heaven and earth.
Let us praise You, and acclaim You, and glorify,
and bless Your holy name,
as it is said:
"A psalm of David. Bless the LORD, O my soul,
and all that is within me bless His holy name!"
O God in the mighty acts of Your power,
great in the glory of Your name;
mighty forever, and awe-inspiring
in the terror of Your deeds.
O King, enthroned on high,
and raised in eminence!
Dwelling in eternity, high and holy is His name!

◄ continue on page 180

וְאַל תִּטְּשֵׁנוּ, יְהֹוָה אֱלֹהֵינוּ, לָנֶצַח.

עַל כֵּן אֵבָרִים שֶׁפִּלַּגְתָּ בָּנוּ

וְרוּחַ וּנְשָׁמָה שֶׁנָּפַחְתָּ בְּאַפֵּנוּ

וְלָשׁוֹן אֲשֶׁר שַׂמְתָּ בְּפִינוּ

הֵן הֵם יוֹדוּ וִיבָרְכוּ וִישַׁבְּחוּ וִיפָאֲרוּ

וִירוֹמְמוּ וְיַעֲרִיצוּ וְיַקְדִּישׁוּ וְיַמְלִיכוּ אֶת שִׁמְךָ מַלְכֵּנוּ

כִּי כָל פֶּה לְךָ יוֹדֶה

וְכָל לָשׁוֹן לְךָ תִשָּׁבַע

וְכָל בֶּרֶךְ לְךָ תִכְרַע

וְכָל קוֹמָה לְפָנֶיךָ תִשְׁתַּחֲוֶה

וְכָל לְבָבוֹת יִירָאוּךָ

וְכָל קֶרֶב וּכְלָיוֹת יְזַמְּרוּ לִשְׁמֶךָ

כַּדָּבָר שֶׁכָּתוּב

כָּל עַצְמֹתַי תֹּאמַרְנָה יְהֹוָה מִי כָמוֹךָ

מַצִּיל עָנִי מֵחָזָק מִמֶּנּוּ, וְעָנִי וְאֶבְיוֹן מִגֹּזְלוֹ:

מִי יִדְמֶה לָּךְ וּמִי יִשְׁוֶה לָּךְ וּמִי יַעֲרָךְ לָךְ

הָאֵל הַגָּדוֹל, הַגִּבּוֹר וְהַנּוֹרָא

אֵל עֶלְיוֹן, קוֹנֵה שָׁמַיִם וָאָרֶץ.

נְהַלֶּלְךָ וּנְשַׁבֵּחֲךָ וּנְפָאֶרְךָ וּנְבָרֵךְ אֶת שֵׁם

קָדְשֶׁךָ

כָּאָמוּר

לְדָוִד, בָּרְכִי נַפְשִׁי אֶת־יְהֹוָה,

וְכָל־קְרָבַי אֶת־שֵׁם קָדְשׁוֹ:

הָאֵל בְּתַעֲצֻמוֹת עֻזֶּךָ

הַגָּדוֹל בִּכְבוֹד שְׁמֶךָ

הַגִּבּוֹר לָנֶצַח וְהַנּוֹרָא בְּנוֹרְאוֹתֶיךָ

הַמֶּלֶךְ הַיּוֹשֵׁב עַל כִּסֵּא.

רָם וְנִשָּׂא

שׁוֹכֵן עַד מָרוֹם וְקָדוֹשׁ שְׁמוֹ

◄ continue on page 181

175

LET US GO AND WALK IN THE LIGHT OF THE LORD

Blessed be the Lord God of Israel.

Halleluya, give praise to the Lord.

Hear my voice in the early morning.
In the early morning I shall rise and appear
    before You,
Our nation resides in your eternal hope.
You girded me with strength for war.
Though I lie down in tears at night, in the
    morning there shall be cries of joy.

The just shall submit in the early morning.
In the early morning I shall call out to You,
    for You are my succor.
I shall rejoice in the early morning over
    Your compassion.

In the early morning they shall go forth and
    in the evening they shall rejoice –
the heavens just before dawn.
May my praise rise before You in the early
    morning.
It shall toil and pass in the early morning.
For in the early morning we put our faith in
    Your compassion.
In the early morning we shall tell of Your
    loving-kindness.

In the early morning I shall do away with
    all the sinners of the land,
You who were born before the morning star.
From the early morning hour till night.

Since the early morning the children of
    Israel have placed their faith in the Lord
That He might hear their prayer.
Perform Your acts of loving-kindness in the
    early morning.

So says the Lord: My judgment shall be
    issued in the early morning.
Faithful servants and prophets in the early
    morning
Shed tears before the heavenly lights.

The horses shall be sanctified in the early
    morning. O Jerusalem
That shines upon their countenances at
    dawn.
For their compassion rises in the early
    morning; and shall endure until the early
    morning.

The works of the Lord are faithful
In the early morning.
For they are like lightning flashing in the
    early morning.
In the early morning the Lord shall pass
    judgment.
On the sixth day at dawn in the early
    morning.

And Moses rose in the early morning.
May the Lord be compassionate, may He
  be indeed.
Take pity on me, for You are wide as the sea
  and who can compare to You
That are like the mighty roaring of the
  waves in the early morning.

Hear my voice.
The Lord is indeed the compassionate One
  rising in the east

Like the sun. Praised be the name of the
  Lord God.
Your countenance appears like the very light
  itself.
Your face flashes in a bank of myriad clouds.
In Your light and righteousness do we have
  light;
For the light in my eyes dims by comparison.

Send forth, therefore, Your light and
  righteousness which has no parallel;

Kes Tesfahun Baruch, Wolleka, 1984

Your right hand and mighty arm and the
 light of Your countenance.
For if the ancestors went down forever
Then no light would ever shine again.
Whereas through the night by the light of
 the fire,
By the light of Your countenance, dear Lord,
 they made their way,
So may they walk forever by the light of
 Your face.
May Your light shine down upon us.
Shine a light upon the righteous,
As the Sabbath is a light unto the world,
So shall You clothe the holy in its light.
Shine a light for the righteous in the
 afterlife,
A light to light my way.

Behold, dear Lord, I suffer, although there
 be no darkness
Before You, even in the afterlife.
Your presence is like a thousand lights, for
 You are the Lord
Who created the heavenly orbs.

May all the stars in heaven sing Your praises,
 along with
The heavenly lights You made for our
 benefit, for they are light.
May they spin in Your waves of light, for
 Your commandments are like light
Upon the earth; and the light of the Lord
 does shine upon our path;
And may there always be light for Your
 chosen ones as the righteous walk

In the light of the sun; and the chosen
 ones proceed by the living light.

And the light shall be brought forth and
 the righteous shall
Find it and death shall pass forever.
The candid light shall grow strong.
His light is a light of justice,
All the lights of heaven shall praise Him
 round about
And a single shining voice shall ring out
To the full extent of the force of light;
By the book of light and the heavenly
 orbs.

For so was it commanded: the first of all
 lights –
Is the sun. And the other spheres shall
 approach, and
The heavenly gates shall be thrown wide,
 and the great light
Whose name is the sun and shines upon
 all others, shall be joined
By the other heavenly lights, those lights
 that are beyond number,
As the Lord said, Let there be light. And
 we shall grow strong in the
Light and the Lord shall cast light upon
 the world, light shall shine upon
Its face, and its light within shall spill
 forth
Like the sunlight and flashing lightning
And all the lights of heaven shall be
 reinforced.

The vision that Ḥanokh the
Righteous scribe beheld.
And the light shall not illuminate in the
heavens but the
Fragrant resting of the light shall serve as
illumination.
What light has there ever been such as this
light?
And behold, a minor light.
I reside beneath the heavens, as light, the
light
That shines in praise of His compassion.

For the ways of the righteous are like light,
and light
Is the way of life of the righteous, they are
light in every instant.

God breathed light into the rain and light
shone forth,
In death there was no light, so the Lord
created light.

Let us go and walk then in the light of the
Lord.

(Eshkoli, 132–133)

For it is written:
"Rejoice in the LORD, O you righteous:
praise is comely to the upright."

By the mouth of the upright You are praised!
By the words of the righteous You are blessed!
By the tongue of the pious You are exalted!
And in the inmost being of the holy You are sanctified!

In the assemblies of the great multitudes
of Your people, the house of Israel,
shall Your name be glorified in joyful song through all generations.
For it is the duty of all creatures who stand before You,
O LORD our God, and God of our fathers,
to offer thanks and praises, and tributes of glory,
to honor, revere, bless, exalt, and adore You;
using all the words of praise and glory
indited by David the son of Yishai, Your anointed servant.

Praised be Your name forever, our King.
God and Ruler, great and holy, in heaven and on earth!
For to You, O LORD our God, and God of our fathers,
song and praise are due: sounds of melody,
acclamations of strength, dominion,
victory, grandeur, and might;
sounds of praise and glory,
ascriptions of holiness and sovereignty,
blessings and thanksgivings, from now and for evermore.
Blessed are You, O LORD, God, King, great in adoration,
God of praises, LORD of wonders,
who makes choice of song and psalm;
O King and God, the Life of all the worlds.

וְכָתוּב
רַנְּנוּ צַדִּיקִים בַּיהוה, לַיְשָׁרִים נָאוָה תְהִלָּה:

בְּפִי יְשָׁרִים תִּתְהַלָּל
וּבְדִבְרֵי צַדִּיקִים תִּתְבָּרַךְ
וּבִלְשׁוֹן חֲסִידִים תִּתְרוֹמָם
וּבְקֶרֶב קְדוֹשִׁים תִּתְקַדָּשׁ

וּבְמַקְהֲלוֹת רִבְבוֹת עַמְּךָ בֵּית יִשְׂרָאֵל
בְּרִנָּה יִתְפָּאַר שִׁמְךָ מַלְכֵּנוּ בְּכָל דּוֹר וָדוֹר
שֶׁכֵּן חוֹבַת כָּל הַיְצוּרִים
לְפָנֶיךָ יהוה אֱלֹהֵינוּ וֵאלֹהֵי אֲבוֹתֵינוּ
לְהוֹדוֹת, לְהַלֵּל,
לְשַׁבֵּחַ, לְפָאֵר,
לְרוֹמֵם, לְהַדֵּר,
לְבָרֵךְ, לְעַלֵּה וּלְקַלֵּס
עַל כָּל דִּבְרֵי שִׁירוֹת וְתִשְׁבְּחוֹת
דָּוִד בֶּן יִשַׁי, עַבְדְּךָ מְשִׁיחֶךָ.

יִשְׁתַּבַּח שִׁמְךָ לָעַד מַלְכֵּנוּ
הָאֵל הַמֶּלֶךְ הַגָּדוֹל וְהַקָּדוֹשׁ בַּשָּׁמַיִם וּבָאָרֶץ
כִּי לְךָ נָאֶה, יהוה אֱלֹהֵינוּ וֵאלֹהֵי אֲבוֹתֵינוּ
שִׁיר וּשְׁבָחָה, הַלֵּל וְזִמְרָה
עֹז וּמֶמְשָׁלָה, נֶצַח, גְּדֻלָּה וּגְבוּרָה
תְּהִלָּה וְתִפְאֶרֶת, קְדֻשָּׁה וּמַלְכוּת
בְּרָכוֹת וְהוֹדָאוֹת, מֵעַתָּה וְעַד עוֹלָם.
בָּרוּךְ אַתָּה יהוה,
אֵל מֶלֶךְ גָּדוֹל בַּתִּשְׁבָּחוֹת
אֵל הַהוֹדָאוֹת אֲדוֹן הַנִּפְלָאוֹת
הַבּוֹחֵר בְּשִׁירֵי זִמְרָה,
מֶלֶךְ, אֵל, חֵי הָעוֹלָמִים.

Prayers in the synagogue in Wolleka, 1976

הִנְנִי מוּכָן וּמְזוּמָן לְקַיֵּם מִצְוַת כּוֹס רְבִיעִי שֶׁל אַרְבַּע כּוֹסוֹת.
לְשֵׁם יִחוּד קוּדְשָׁא בְּרִיךְ הוּא וּשְׁכִינְתֵּיהּ עַל יְדֵי הַהוּא טָמִיר וְנֶעְלָם בְּשֵׁם כָּל יִשְׂרָאֵל.

בָּרוּךְ אַתָּה יהוה אֱלֹהֵינוּ מֶלֶךְ הָעוֹלָם בּוֹרֵא פְּרִי הַגָּפֶן.

שׁוֹתִים כּוֹס רְבִיעִי בַּהֲסִבַּת שְׂמֹאל.

בָּרוּךְ אַתָּה יהוה אֱלֹהֵינוּ מֶלֶךְ הָעוֹלָם, עַל הַגֶּפֶן וְעַל פְּרִי הַגֶּפֶן וְעַל תְּנוּבַת הַשָּׂדֶה וְעַל אֶרֶץ חֶמְדָּה טוֹבָה וּרְחָבָה, שֶׁרָצִיתָ וְהִנְחַלְתָּ לַאֲבוֹתֵינוּ לֶאֱכֹל מִפִּרְיָהּ וְלִשְׂבֹּעַ מִטּוּבָהּ. רַחֵם נָא יהוה אֱלֹהֵינוּ עַל יִשְׂרָאֵל עַמֶּךָ וְעַל יְרוּשָׁלַיִם עִירֶךָ וְעַל צִיּוֹן מִשְׁכַּן כְּבוֹדֶךָ וְעַל מִזְבְּחֶךָ וְעַל הֵיכָלֶךָ. וּבְנֵה יְרוּשָׁלַיִם עִיר הַקֹּדֶשׁ בִּמְהֵרָה בְיָמֵינוּ, וְהַעֲלֵנוּ לְתוֹכָהּ וְשַׂמְּחֵנוּ בְּבִנְיָנָהּ וְנֹאכַל מִפִּרְיָהּ וְנִשְׂבַּע מִטּוּבָהּ, וּנְבָרֶכְךָ עָלֶיהָ בִּקְדֻשָּׁה וּבְטָהֳרָה. (בשבת: וּרְצֵה וְהַחֲלִיצֵנוּ בְּיוֹם הַשַּׁבָּת הַזֶּה) וְשַׂמְּחֵנוּ בְּיוֹם חַג הַמַּצּוֹת הַזֶּה כִּי אַתָּה יהוה טוֹב וּמֵטִיב לַכֹּל, וְנוֹדֶה לְּךָ עַל הָאָרֶץ וְעַל פְּרִי הַגָּפֶן/ אם היין מארץ ישראל: גַּפְנָהּ/. בָּרוּךְ אַתָּה יהוה עַל הָאָרֶץ וְעַל פְּרִי הַגָּפֶן/ אם היין מארץ ישראל: גַּפְנָהּ/.

I am hereby prepared and ready to fulfill the commandment of the fourth of the four cups. For the sake of the unification of the Holy One, blessed be He, and His Divine Presence, through that which is hidden and concealed, in the name of all Israel.

Blessed are You, LORD our God, King of the Universe, who creates fruit of the vine.

Drink the fourth cup while reclining to the left.

Blessed are You, LORD our God, King of the Universe, for the nourishment and sustenance and for the vine and the fruit of the vine. and for the produce of the field; for the desirable, good and spacious land that You willingly gave as heritage to our ancestors, that they might eat of its fruit and be satisfied with its goodness. Have compassion, LORD our God, on Israel Your people, on Jerusalem, Your city, on Zion the home of Your glory, on Your altar and Your Temple. May You rebuild Jerusalem, the holy city swiftly in our time, and may You bring us back there, rejoicing in its rebuilding, eating from its fruit, satisfied by its goodness, and blessing You for it in holiness and purity. (*On Shabbat:* Be pleased to refresh us on this Sabbath Day.) Grant us joy on this Festival of Matzot. For You, God, are good and do good to all and we thank You for the land and for the fruit of the vine. Blessed are You, LORD, for the land and for the fruit of the vine. and for the nourishment and for the fruit of the vine. Blessed are You, LORD, for the land and for the nourishment and the fruit of the vine.

HEAR MY PRAYER, MY LORD

O Lord God of Abraham, Isaac and Jacob,
You who entered an eternal covenant with
    their offspring;
God of Moses and Aaron,
Who made His voice known to them on
    Mount Sinai,
And commanded them to lead the children
    of Israel.

O Lord, God of the priests, the prophets
And the holy ones, God of Daniel, Ḥanania,
Mishael and Azarya, your faithful servants,
Who had faith in the Lord and were
    answered,
I too am Your faithful servant.

As I call out Your name,
As I speak out Your praise,
Hear my prayer dear Lord,
May You receive these words from my lips,
For I have put my faith in You.

(Wurmbrand)

Kes Menashe Zimro, Sigd Holiday, Addis Ababa, 1990

183

חֲסַל סִדּוּר פֶּסַח כְּהִלְכָתוֹ, כְּכָל מִשְׁפָּטוֹ וְחֻקָּתוֹ
כַּאֲשֶׁר זָכִינוּ לְסַדֵּר אוֹתוֹ, כֵּן נִזְכֶּה לַעֲשׂוֹתוֹ
זָךְ שׁוֹכֵן מְעוֹנָה, קוֹמֵם קְהַל עֲדַת מִי מָנָה
קָרֵב נַהֵל נִטְעֵי כַנָּה, פְּדוּיִים לְצִיּוֹן בְּרִנָּה.

לְשָׁנָה הַבָּאָה בִּירוּשָׁלַיִם הַבְּנוּיָה.

CONCLUSION

Concluded in due form is our Pesaḥ-night service,
in all its regulations and precepts.
As it was our privilege to celebrate it this night,
so may we be found worthy to celebrate it in time to come.
O You Pure One, who dwells in heaven,
raise up the assembly of Your people innumerable!
Shortly lead them – called "the plant of Your vine" –
in freedom to Zion with a joyful shout.

NEXT YEAR IN JERUSALEM THE REBUILT!

Kes Jacob Zeru, 1937

Abba Tegenye Demelaw, Gondar, 2008

RISE UP, JERUSALEM

Halleluya, give praise to the Lord:
Rise up, Jerusalem:
May your walls be rebuilt, O Jerusalem:
O the gates of Jerusalem:

I shall turn to You in prayer in Jerusalem:
In the streets of Jerusalem:

Sitting in judgment in Jerusalem:
In the midst of Jerusalem:

Raise up the light of Jerusalem:
May you be settled, O Jerusalem:

May their blood be spilled around Jerusalem:
Hear, O Jerusalem:

Your praise rises in the midst of Jerusalem:
Your heart mourns, O Jerusalem:

Your charms, O Jerusalem:
Sit still, in praise, O Jerusalem:

May Jerusalem be blessed with peace:
That the nations of the world might know,
   O Jerusalem:

Behold the splendor of Jerusalem:
Recall the nation of Jerusalem:

Residing in the midst of Jerusalem:
Raised in Jerusalem:

I have not forgotten thee, Jerusalem:
And I shall tread the paths of Jerusalem:

On the day of Jerusalem:
The holy Jerusalem:

May Jerusalem be praised:
The cities of Jerusalem:

The city of our forefathers, O Jerusalem:
The strength of Judea, O Jerusalem:

The holy Jerusalem:
Jerusalem that has been scorned:

Seat of the sacred, O Jerusalem:
Those who reside in Jerusalem:

Slow to anger in Jerusalem:
The homes of Jerusalem:

In your city, Jerusalem:
The gates of Jerusalem:

Angels and singers, O Jerusalem:
The homes of Jerusalem:

And in the word, Jerusalem:
The stones of Jerusalem:

Lament for Jerusalem:
Shed tears unto Jerusalem:

We shall yet behold Jerusalem:
The word of Jerusalem:

The holy mount, Jerusalem:
Those exiled from Jerusalem:

Those who waged war against Jerusalem:
The tribe of Judah, O Jerusalem:

All that has been spoken by Jerusalem:
Her paths, fair Jerusalem:

We have come unto Jerusalem:
Her iniquities, O Jerusalem:

Unto thee, Jerusalem:
All those who recall Jerusalem:

The entire nation, Jerusalem:
Worship in Jerusalem:

Before the gates of Jerusalem:
We shall worship, O Jerusalem:

The entire army of Jerusalem:
Shall sing of her, Jerusalem:

Your dear walls, Jerusalem:
We shall bless Jerusalem:

She has fallen, O Jerusalem:
She has succumbed, O Jerusalem:

As they took you, O Jerusalem:
The one who deciphers all secrets,
    O Jerusalem:

My light, Jerusalem:

The House of the Lord, Jerusalem.

(Eshkoli, 139–140)

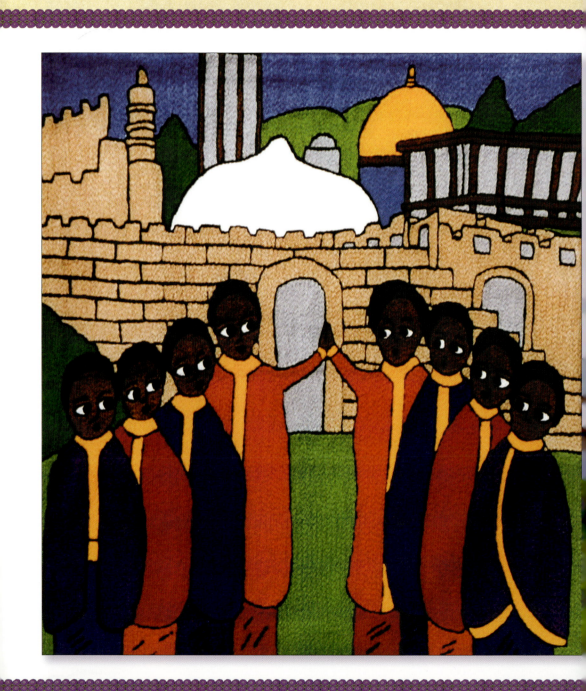

TO THE STORK

Once a year, as winter approaches, flocks of storks
   arrive in Ethiopia from Europe after passing through
   the land of Israel.
The members of the community had the custom of
   turning their eyes heavenward to these birds and
   inquiring:

"*Shimeila, shimeila, ageirachin Eiyeirusalem deiheina?*"
O stork, stork, what is the state of our land Jerusalem?

בחוץ לארץ אומרים פיוט זה רק בלילה הראשון של פסח.

וּבְכֵן וַיְהִי בַּחֲצִי הַלָּיְלָה

בַּלָּיְלָה	אָז רֹב נִסִּים הִפְלֵאתָ
הַלָּיְלָה	בְּרֹאשׁ אַשְׁמוּרוֹת זֶה
לָיְלָה	גֵּר צֶדֶק נִצַּחְתּוֹ, כְּנֶחֱלַק לוֹ

וַיְהִי בַּחֲצִי הַלָּיְלָה

הַלָּיְלָה	דַּנְתָּ מֶלֶךְ גְּרָר בַּחֲלוֹם
לָיְלָה	הִפְחַדְתָּ אֲרַמִּי בְּאֶמֶשׁ
לָיְלָה	וַיָּשַׂר יִשְׂרָאֵל לְאֵל, וַיּוּכַל לוֹ

וַיְהִי בַּחֲצִי הַלָּיְלָה

הַלָּיְלָה	זֶרַע בְּכוֹרֵי פַתְרוֹס מָחַצְתָּ בַּחֲצִי
בַּלָּיְלָה	חֵילָם לֹא מָצְאוּ בְּקוּמָם
לָיְלָה	טִיסַת נְגִיד חֲרֹשֶׁת סִלִּיתָ בְּכוֹכְבֵי

וַיְהִי בַּחֲצִי הַלָּיְלָה

In the Diaspora, this poem is recited on the first night of the festival only.

AND IT ALL HAPPENED AT MIDNIGHT

A host of miracles You did perform   *at midnight*
Beginning with our father Abraham   *at midnight*
Captives he took in fight with monarchs four   *at midnight*
     And it all happened at midnight

Dreams You did send to warn the king of Gerar   *at midnight*
Eerie the visions that to Laban came   *at midnight*
Fiercely fought Jacob with an angel grim   *at midnight*
     And it all happened at midnight

Great was the slaughter of the firstborn host   *at midnight*
Heavy the loss the Egyptians felt   *at midnight*
Infinite the stars that fought against Sisera's host   *at midnight*
     And it all happened at midnight

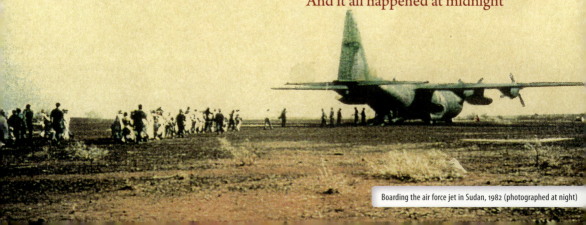

Boarding the air force jet in Sudan, 1982 (photographed at night)

יַעַץ מְחָרֵף לְנוֹפֵף אִוּוּי, הוֹבַשְׁתָּ פְגָרָיו   בַּלַּיְלָה
כָּרַע בֵּל וּמַצָּבוֹ בְּאִישׁוֹן   לַיְלָה
לְאִישׁ חֲמוּדוֹת נִגְלָה רָז חֲזוֹת   לַיְלָה
וַיְהִי בַּחֲצִי הַלַּיְלָה

מִשְׁתַּכֵּר בִּכְלֵי קֹדֶשׁ נֶהֱרַג בּוֹ   בַּלַּיְלָה
נוֹשַׁע מִבּוֹר אֲרָיוֹת, פּוֹתֵר בְּעִתּוּתֵי   לַיְלָה
שִׂנְאָה נָטַר אֲגָגִי, וְכָתַב סְפָרִים   בַּלַּיְלָה
וַיְהִי בַּחֲצִי הַלַּיְלָה

עוֹרַרְתָּ נִצְחֲךָ עָלָיו בְּנֶדֶד שְׁנַת   לַיְלָה
פּוּרָה תִדְרֹךְ לְשׁוֹמֵר מַה   מִלַּיְלָה
צָרַח כַּשּׁוֹמֵר, וְשָׂח אָתָא בֹקֶר וְגַם   לַיְלָה
וַיְהִי בַּחֲצִי הַלַּיְלָה

קָרֵב יוֹם אֲשֶׁר הוּא לֹא יוֹם וְלֹא   לַיְלָה
רָם הוֹדַע כִּי לְךָ הַיּוֹם אַף לְךָ   הַלַּיְלָה
שׁוֹמְרִים הַפְקֵד לְעִירְךָ כָּל הַיּוֹם וְכָל   הַלַּיְלָה
תָּאִיר כְּאוֹר יוֹם חֶשְׁכַּת   לַיְלָה
וַיְהִי בַּחֲצִי הַלַּיְלָה

Just was the slaughter of the Ashshurian foe   at midnight
Knocked down was Bel and shattered quite   at midnight
Laid bare to Daniel were the secret things   at midnight
    And it all happened at midnight

Midst drunken toasts was slain a king   at midnight
No mystic sign nonplussed the pious youth   at midnight
Out sent the Agagite his hateful charge   at midnight
    And it all happened at midnight

Perplexed and sleepless was his royal Lord   at midnight
Quickly the winepress tread, and hail the watch   at midnight
Reply comes from the watchman, "See, the dawn!"   at midnight
    And it all happened at midnight

Soon come that day of which the prophets spoke   at midnight
Yours is the day, and Yours the night, proclaim   at midnight
Upon the city newly built set watch   at midnight
Victoriously give light to us Your flock forlorn,
Who seek You all the night, and wait for dawn!

    And it all happened at midnight

The Journey to the Land of Israel

by Haim Idisis

The moon watches over from above,
Over the poor sack of food we have,
The desert lies beneath me, with no end in
   sight
And my mother promises my younger
   siblings in the night:

Just a little more, just another little bit,
Lift your feet my children,
One last push before we reach Jerusalem.

Light of the moon, be strong,
Our sack of food did not last long,
The desert never ends, and the jackals raise
   their cry,
While my mother calms my younger siblings
   in the night:

Just a little more, just another little bit,
Soon we shall be redeemed as well,

For we shall not cease till we reach the land
   of Israel.

Yet in the night, the thieves attacked,
With knives and sharp swords they came.
The blood of my mother runs in the desert,
   the moon is my witness,
And I promise my younger siblings:

Just a little more, just another little bit,
The dream will finally come true,
In a little while we shall reach the land of
   Israel.

By the light of the moon I see my mother's
   figure
Staring at me. Dear mother, do not
   disappear;
If she were by my side, she could
Convince them that I too am a Jew.

Just a little more, just another little bit,
Lift up your eyes my children,
One last push before we reach Jerusalem.

(Mizmor, 54)

The refugee camp near Gedaref, Sudan, 1983

In the Diaspora, this poem is recited on the second night of the festival only.

**SO YOU MAY SAY, "THIS IS THE DAY,
THE PESAḤ OFFERING TO SLAY."**

A mighty strength You did display	on Pesaḥ
Beyond all feasts You raise the day	of Pesaḥ
Complete to Abraham the tale foretold	of Pesaḥ

So you may say, "This is the day, The Pesaḥ offering to slay."

Divine the guests who come that day	of Pesaḥ
Entered his tent and ate the bread	of Pesaḥ
For them he slew a tender calf	on Pesaḥ

So you may say, "This is the day, The Pesaḥ offering to slay."

Grim on Sodom He rained His fire	on Pesaḥ
He saved but one who baked the cakes	of Pesaḥ
Ill-fated was that Egyptian land	on Pesaḥ

So you may say, "This is the day, The Pesaḥ offering to slay."

Judgment befell each eldest son	on Pesaḥ
Kindly reprieved were Israel's sons	on Pesaḥ
Left unmolested on that night	of Pesaḥ

So you may say, "This is the day, The Pesaḥ offering to slay."

Mighty Jericho was breached and won	on Pesaḥ
Next Midian charged by barley cake	on Pesaḥ
Over our foes a fiery bolt	on Pesaḥ

So you may say, "This is the day, The Pesaḥ offering to slay."

Past Nov, Ashshur shall not set foot	till Pesaḥ
Quick on the wall the writ of doom	on Pesaḥ
Regaled with food the table spread	on Pesaḥ

So you may say, "This is the day, The Pesaḥ offering to slay."

She called a three day fast for all	on Pesaḥ
Then Haman high You did dispatch	on Pesaḥ
Upon Edom two things shall fall	of Pesaḥ
Victoriously uplift Your arm, to save us all, from every harm,	on Pesaḥ

So you may say, "This is the day, The Pesaḥ offering to slay."

בחוץ לארץ אומרים פיוט זה רק בלילה השני של פסח.

וּבְכֵן וַאֲמַרְתֶּם זֶבַח פֶּסַח

אֹמֶץ גְּבוּרוֹתֶיךָ הִפְלֵאתָ   בַּפֶּסַח
בְּרֹאשׁ כָּל מוֹעֲדוֹת נִשֵּׂאתָ   פֶּסַח
גִּלִּיתָ לְאֶזְרָחִי חֲצוֹת לֵיל   פֶּסַח

וַאֲמַרְתֶּם זֶבַח פֶּסַח

דְּלָתָיו דָּפַקְתָּ כְּחֹם הַיּוֹם   בַּפֶּסַח
הִסְעִיד נוֹצְצִים עֻגוֹת מַצּוֹת   בַּפֶּסַח
וְאֶל הַבָּקָר, רָץ זֵכֶר לְשׁוֹר עֵרֶךְ   פֶּסַח

וַאֲמַרְתֶּם זֶבַח פֶּסַח

זֹעֲמוּ סְדוֹמִים, וְלֹהֲטוּ בָּאֵשׁ   בַּפֶּסַח
חֻלַּץ לוֹט מֵהֶם, וּמַצּוֹת אָפָה בְּקֵץ   פֶּסַח
טֵאטֵאתָ אַדְמַת מֹף וְנֹף בְּעָבְרְךָ   בַּפֶּסַח

וַאֲמַרְתֶּם זֶבַח פֶּסַח

יָהּ, רֹאשׁ כָּל אוֹן מָחַצְתָּ בְּלֵיל שִׁמּוּר   פֶּסַח
כַּבִּיר, עַל בֵּן בְּכוֹר פָּסַחְתָּ בְּדַם   פֶּסַח
לְבִלְתִּי תֵּת מַשְׁחִית לָבֹא בִּפְתָחַי   בַּפֶּסַח

וַאֲמַרְתֶּם זֶבַח פֶּסַח

מְסֻגֶּרֶת סֻגָּרָה בְּעִתּוֹתֵי   פֶּסַח
נִשְׁמְדָה מִדְיָן בִּצְלִיל שְׂעוֹרֵי עֹמֶר   פֶּסַח
שֹׂרְפוּ מִשְׁמַנֵּי פּוּל וְלוּד, בִּיקַד יְקוֹד   פֶּסַח

וַאֲמַרְתֶּם זֶבַח פֶּסַח

עוֹד הַיּוֹם בְּנֹב לַעֲמֹד, עַד גָּעָה עוֹנַת   פֶּסַח
פַּס יָד כָּתְבָה לְקַעֲקֵעַ צוּל   בַּפֶּסַח
צָפֹה הַצָּפִית עָרוֹךְ הַשֻּׁלְחָן   בַּפֶּסַח

וַאֲמַרְתֶּם זֶבַח פֶּסַח

קָהָל כִּנְּסָה הֲדַסָּה, צוֹם לְשַׁלֵּשׁ   בַּפֶּסַח
רֹאשׁ מִבֵּית רָשָׁע מָחַצְתָּ בְּעֵץ חֲמִשִּׁים   בַּפֶּסַח
שְׁתֵּי אֵלֶּה, רֶגַע תָּבִיא לְעוּצִית   בַּפֶּסַח
תָּעֹז יָדְךָ, תָּרוּם יְמִינֶךָ, כְּלֵיל הִתְקַדֶּשׁ חַג   פֶּסַח

וַאֲמַרְתֶּם זֶבַח פֶּסַח

HIS THE GLORY AND HIS THE MILDNESS

Powerful in royalty / Gentle like the ways of the Law;
What is it that His angels say to Him?
Yours, and again, Yours; Yours and still more Yours; Yours and only Yours;
Yours is the kingdom: His the glory; And His the mildness!

Famous in royalty / Beautiful like the ways of the Law;
What is it that His faithful servants say to Him?
Yours, and again, Yours; Yours and still more Yours; Yours and only Yours;
Yours is the kingdom: His the glory; And His the mildness!

Stainless in sovereignty / Strong like the ways of the Law;
What is it that His secretary-angels say to Him?
Yours, and again, Yours; Yours and still more Yours; Yours and only Yours;
Yours is the kingdom: His the glory; And His the mildness!

Single in sovereignty / Unchallenged like the ways of the Law;
What is it that His scholars say to Him?
Yours, and again, Yours; Yours and still more Yours; Yours and only Yours;
Yours is the kingdom: His the glory; And His the mildness!

Sublime in royalty / Commanding fear like the ways of the Law;
What is it that His clustering angels say to Him?
Yours, and again, Yours; Yours and still more Yours; Yours and only Yours;
Yours is the kingdom: His the glory; And His the mildness!

Humble in royalty / Saving us like the ways of the Law;
What is it that His righteous ones say to Him?
Yours, and again, Yours; Yours and still more Yours; Yours and only Yours;
Yours is the kingdom: His the glory; And His the mildness!

Holy in royalty / Merciful like the ways of the Law;
What is it that His innumerable angels say to Him?
Yours, and again, Yours; Yours and still more Yours; Yours and only Yours;
Yours is the kingdom: His the glory; And His the mildness!

Indomitable in royalty / Gently aiding us like the ways of the Law;
What is it that His innocent ones say to Him?
Yours, and again, Yours; Yours and still more Yours; Yours and only Yours;
Yours is the kingdom: His the glory; And His the mildness!

כִּי לוֹ נָאֶה, כִּי לוֹ יָאֶה

אַדִּיר בִּמְלוּכָה   בָּחוּר כַּהֲלָכָה   גְּדוּדָיו יֹאמְרוּ לוֹ
לְךָ וּלְךָ, לְךָ כִּי לְךָ, לְךָ אַף לְךָ, לְךָ יהוה הַמַּמְלָכָה
כִּי לוֹ נָאֶה, כִּי לוֹ יָאֶה

דָּגוּל בִּמְלוּכָה   הָדוּר כַּהֲלָכָה   וָתִיקָיו יֹאמְרוּ לוֹ
לְךָ וּלְךָ, לְךָ כִּי לְךָ, לְךָ אַף לְךָ, לְךָ יהוה הַמַּמְלָכָה
כִּי לוֹ נָאֶה, כִּי לוֹ יָאֶה

זַכַּאי בִּמְלוּכָה   חָסִין כַּהֲלָכָה   טַפְסְרָיו יֹאמְרוּ לוֹ
לְךָ וּלְךָ, לְךָ כִּי לְךָ, לְךָ אַף לְךָ, לְךָ יהוה הַמַּמְלָכָה
כִּי לוֹ נָאֶה, כִּי לוֹ יָאֶה

יָחִיד בִּמְלוּכָה   כַּבִּיר כַּהֲלָכָה   לִמּוּדָיו יֹאמְרוּ לוֹ
לְךָ וּלְךָ, לְךָ כִּי לְךָ, לְךָ אַף לְךָ, לְךָ יהוה הַמַּמְלָכָה
כִּי לוֹ נָאֶה, כִּי לוֹ יָאֶה

מֶלֶךְ בִּמְלוּכָה   נוֹרָא כַּהֲלָכָה   סְבִיבָיו יֹאמְרוּ לוֹ
לְךָ וּלְךָ, לְךָ כִּי לְךָ, לְךָ אַף לְךָ, לְךָ יהוה הַמַּמְלָכָה
כִּי לוֹ נָאֶה, כִּי לוֹ יָאֶה

עָנָו בִּמְלוּכָה   פּוֹדֶה כַּהֲלָכָה   צַדִּיקָיו יֹאמְרוּ לוֹ
לְךָ וּלְךָ, לְךָ כִּי לְךָ, לְךָ אַף לְךָ, לְךָ יהוה הַמַּמְלָכָה
כִּי לוֹ נָאֶה, כִּי לוֹ יָאֶה

קָדוֹשׁ בִּמְלוּכָה   רַחוּם כַּהֲלָכָה   שִׁנְאַנָּיו יֹאמְרוּ לוֹ
לְךָ וּלְךָ, לְךָ כִּי לְךָ, לְךָ אַף לְךָ, לְךָ יהוה הַמַּמְלָכָה
כִּי לוֹ נָאֶה, כִּי לוֹ יָאֶה

תַּקִּיף בִּמְלוּכָה   תּוֹמֵךְ כַּהֲלָכָה   תְּמִימָיו יֹאמְרוּ לוֹ
לְךָ וּלְךָ, לְךָ כִּי לְךָ, לְךָ אַף לְךָ, לְךָ יהוה הַמַּמְלָכָה
כִּי לוֹ נָאֶה, כִּי לוֹ יָאֶה

THE LORD IS ONE

The Lord is One.

The Lord our God is One.

The Lord our King is One.

The Lord our Creator is One.

The Lord our Guardian is One.

The Lord our Shepherd is One.

The Lord we praise is One.

The Lord, our source of happiness and joy, is One.

The Lord we exalt is One.

The Lord on high is One.

The awesome Lord is One.

The Lord is faithful,

The Lord redeems,

The Lord is mighty,

The Lord is good,

The Lord is strong,

The Lord avenges,

The Lord is powerful,

The Lord protects,

The Lord is slow to anger and full of loving-kindness and truth, He shall not afflict forever nor be angry eternally.

Show compassion to those You did not previously pity and forgive those You have not forgiven until now.
O Lord
Your name is compassion forever after.

The Lord God is the Lord of lords.

The Lord God is the King of kings.

The Lord God is the Master of all masters.

The Lord God is the Ruler over all rulers.

The Lord God is One.

(Halévy, 11–12)

בחוץ לארץ, סופרים את העומר (עמ׳ 212) בלילה השני.

אַדִּיר הוּא

יִבְנֶה בֵּיתוֹ בְּקָרוֹב

בִּמְהֵרָה בִּמְהֵרָה, בְּיָמֵינוּ בְּקָרוֹב

בְּנֵה בֵיתְךָ בְּקָרוֹב	אֵל בְּנֵה	אֵל בְּנֵה
דָּגוּל הוּא	גָּדוֹל הוּא	בָּחוּר הוּא
זַכַּאי הוּא	וָתִיק הוּא	הָדוּר הוּא
יָחִיד הוּא	טָהוֹר הוּא	חָסִיד הוּא
מֶלֶךְ הוּא	לָמוּד הוּא	כַּבִּיר הוּא
עִזּוּז הוּא	שַׂגִּיב הוּא	נוֹרָא הוּא
קָדוֹשׁ הוּא	צַדִּיק הוּא	פּוֹדֶה הוּא
תַּקִּיף הוּא	שַׁדַּי הוּא	רַחוּם הוּא

יִבְנֶה בֵּיתוֹ בְּקָרוֹב

בִּמְהֵרָה בִּמְהֵרָה, בְּיָמֵינוּ בְּקָרוֹב

אֵל בְּנֵה   אֵל בְּנֵה

בְּנֵה בֵיתְךָ בְּקָרוֹב

In the Diaspora, on the second night the Omer is counted here (page 212).

MIGHTY IS HE,

Let Him rebuild His House, Rebuild it soon.
In our time, in our time: soon, O soon!
O God, build, O build; rebuild Your House soon!

BLESSED,	GREAT,	RENOWNED,
EXCELLENT,	FAMOUS,	PURE,
PIOUS,	CLEAN,	UNIQUE,
POWERFUL,	SAGE,	ROYAL,
FEARFUL,	EMINENT,	STRONG,
READY TO SAVE,	JUST,	HOLY,
MERCIFUL,	MIGHTY,	STRONG IS HE,

Let Him rebuild His House, Rebuild it soon.
In our time, in our time: soon, O soon!
O God, build, O build;

REBUILD YOUR HOUSE SOON!

WHO KNOWS ONE?
I KNOW ONE.
OUR GOD IS ONE
IN HEAVEN AND EARTH.

Who knows two?
I know two.
The tablets of the covenant are two.
Our God is One in heaven and earth.

Who knows three?
I know three.
The patriarchs are three.
The tablets are two.
Our God is One in heaven and earth.

Who knows four?
I know four.
The matriarchs are four.
The patriarchs are three.
The tablets are two.
Our God is One in heaven and earth.

Who knows five?
I know five.
The books of the Torah are five.
The matriarchs are four.
The patriarchs are three.
The tablets are two.
Our God is One in heaven and earth.

אֶחָד מִי יוֹדֵעַ

אֶחָד אֲנִי יוֹדֵעַ

אֶחָד אֱלֹהֵינוּ שֶׁבַּשָּׁמַיִם וּבָאָרֶץ

שְׁנַיִם מִי יוֹדֵעַ
שְׁנַיִם אֲנִי יוֹדֵעַ
שְׁנֵי לוּחוֹת הַבְּרִית
אֶחָד אֱלֹהֵינוּ שֶׁבַּשָּׁמַיִם וּבָאָרֶץ

שְׁלוֹשָׁה מִי יוֹדֵעַ
שְׁלוֹשָׁה אֲנִי יוֹדֵעַ
שְׁלוֹשָׁה אָבוֹת
שְׁנֵי לוּחוֹת הַבְּרִית
אֶחָד אֱלֹהֵינוּ שֶׁבַּשָּׁמַיִם וּבָאָרֶץ

אַרְבַּע מִי יוֹדֵעַ
אַרְבַּע אֲנִי יוֹדֵעַ
אַרְבַּע אִמָּהוֹת
שְׁלוֹשָׁה אָבוֹת   שְׁנֵי לוּחוֹת הַבְּרִית
אֶחָד אֱלֹהֵינוּ שֶׁבַּשָּׁמַיִם וּבָאָרֶץ

חֲמִשָּׁה מִי יוֹדֵעַ
חֲמִשָּׁה אֲנִי יוֹדֵעַ
חֲמִשָּׁה חֻמְשֵׁי תוֹרָה
אַרְבַּע אִמָּהוֹת   שְׁלוֹשָׁה אָבוֹת   שְׁנֵי לוּחוֹת הַבְּרִית
אֶחָד אֱלֹהֵינוּ שֶׁבַּשָּׁמַיִם וּבָאָרֶץ

Who knows six?
I know six.
The orders of the Mishna are six.
The books of the Torah are five. The matriarchs are four.
The patriarchs are three.
The tablets are two.
Our God is One in heaven and earth.

Who knows seven?
I know seven.
The days of the week are seven.
The orders of the Mishna are six. The books of the Torah are five.
The matriarchs are four. The patriarchs are three.
The tablets are two.
Our God is One in heaven and earth.

Who knows eight?
I know eight.
The days for circumcision are eight.
The days of the week are seven.
The orders of the Mishna are six. The books of the Torah are five.
The matriarchs are four. The patriarchs are three.
The tablets are two.
Our God is One in heaven and earth.

Who knows nine?
I know nine.
The months for childbirth are nine.
The days for circumcision are eight.
The days of the week are seven.
The orders of the Mishna are six. The books of the Torah are five.
The matriarchs are four. The patriarchs are three.
The tablets are two.
Our God is One in heaven and earth.

שִׁשָּׁה מִי יוֹדֵעַ

שִׁשָּׁה אֲנִי יוֹדֵעַ

שִׁשָּׁה סִדְרֵי מִשְׁנָה

חֲמִשָּׁה חֻמְשֵׁי תוֹרָה   אַרְבַּע אִמָּהוֹת   שְׁלוֹשָׁה אָבוֹת

שְׁנֵי לוּחוֹת הַבְּרִית

אֶחָד אֱלֹהֵינוּ שֶׁבַּשָּׁמַיִם וּבָאָרֶץ

שִׁבְעָה מִי יוֹדֵעַ

שִׁבְעָה אֲנִי יוֹדֵעַ

שִׁבְעָה יְמֵי שַׁבַּתָּא

שִׁשָּׁה סִדְרֵי מִשְׁנָה   חֲמִשָּׁה חֻמְשֵׁי תוֹרָה

אַרְבַּע אִמָּהוֹת   שְׁלוֹשָׁה אָבוֹת   שְׁנֵי לוּחוֹת הַבְּרִית

אֶחָד אֱלֹהֵינוּ שֶׁבַּשָּׁמַיִם וּבָאָרֶץ

שְׁמוֹנָה מִי יוֹדֵעַ

שְׁמוֹנָה אֲנִי יוֹדֵעַ

שְׁמוֹנָה יְמֵי מִילָה

שִׁבְעָה יְמֵי שַׁבַּתָּא   שִׁשָּׁה סִדְרֵי מִשְׁנָה

חֲמִשָּׁה חֻמְשֵׁי תוֹרָה   אַרְבַּע אִמָּהוֹת   שְׁלוֹשָׁה אָבוֹת

שְׁנֵי לוּחוֹת הַבְּרִית

אֶחָד אֱלֹהֵינוּ שֶׁבַּשָּׁמַיִם וּבָאָרֶץ

תִּשְׁעָה מִי יוֹדֵעַ

תִּשְׁעָה אֲנִי יוֹדֵעַ

תִּשְׁעָה יַרְחֵי לֵדָה

שְׁמוֹנָה יְמֵי מִילָה   שִׁבְעָה יְמֵי שַׁבַּתָּא

שִׁשָּׁה סִדְרֵי מִשְׁנָה   חֲמִשָּׁה חֻמְשֵׁי תוֹרָה

אַרְבַּע אִמָּהוֹת   שְׁלוֹשָׁה אָבוֹת   שְׁנֵי לוּחוֹת הַבְּרִית

אֶחָד אֱלֹהֵינוּ שֶׁבַּשָּׁמַיִם וּבָאָרֶץ

Who knows ten?
I know ten.
The words from Sinai are ten.
The months for childbirth are nine.
The days for circumcision are eight. The days of the week are seven.
The orders of the Mishna are six. The books of the Torah are five.
The matriarchs are four.
The patriarchs are three.
The tablets are two.
Our God is One in heaven and earth.

Who knows eleven?
I know eleven.
The stars of Joseph's dream are eleven.
The words from Sinai are ten. The months for childbirth are nine.
The days for circumcision are eight. The days of the week are seven.
The orders of the Mishna are six. The books of the Torah are five.
The matriarchs are four.
The patriarchs are three.
The tablets are two.
Our God is One in heaven and earth.

Who knows twelve?
I know twelve.
The tribes of Israel are twelve.
The stars of Joseph's dream are eleven.
The words from Sinai are ten. The months for childbirth are nine.
The days for circumcision are eight. The days of the week are seven.
The orders of the Mishna are six. The books of the Torah are five.
The matriarchs are four.
The patriarchs are three.
The tablets are two.
Our God is One in heaven and earth.

עֲשָׂרָה מִי יוֹדֵעַ

עֲשָׂרָה אֲנִי יוֹדֵעַ

עֲשָׂרָה דִבְּרַיָּא

תִּשְׁעָה יַרְחֵי לֵדָה   שְׁמוֹנָה יְמֵי מִילָה
שִׁבְעָה יְמֵי שַׁבַּתָּא   שִׁשָּׁה סִדְרֵי מִשְׁנָה
חֲמִשָּׁה חֻמְשֵׁי תוֹרָה   אַרְבַּע אִמָּהוֹת   שְׁלוֹשָׁה אָבוֹת
שְׁנֵי לוּחוֹת הַבְּרִית
אֶחָד אֱלֹהֵינוּ שֶׁבַּשָּׁמַיִם וּבָאָרֶץ

אַחַד עָשָׂר מִי יוֹדֵעַ

אַחַד עָשָׂר אֲנִי יוֹדֵעַ

אַחַד עָשָׂר כּוֹכְבַיָּא

עֲשָׂרָה דִבְּרַיָּא   תִּשְׁעָה יַרְחֵי לֵדָה
שְׁמוֹנָה יְמֵי מִילָה   שִׁבְעָה יְמֵי שַׁבַּתָּא
שִׁשָּׁה סִדְרֵי מִשְׁנָה   חֲמִשָּׁה חֻמְשֵׁי תוֹרָה
אַרְבַּע אִמָּהוֹת   שְׁלוֹשָׁה אָבוֹת   שְׁנֵי לוּחוֹת הַבְּרִית
אֶחָד אֱלֹהֵינוּ שֶׁבַּשָּׁמַיִם וּבָאָרֶץ

שְׁנֵים עָשָׂר מִי יוֹדֵעַ

שְׁנֵים עָשָׂר אֲנִי יוֹדֵעַ

שְׁנֵים עָשָׂר שִׁבְטַיָּא

אַחַד עָשָׂר כּוֹכְבַיָּא   עֲשָׂרָה דִבְּרַיָּא   תִּשְׁעָה יַרְחֵי לֵדָה
שְׁמוֹנָה יְמֵי מִילָה   שִׁבְעָה יְמֵי שַׁבַּתָּא
שִׁשָּׁה סִדְרֵי מִשְׁנָה   חֲמִשָּׁה חֻמְשֵׁי תוֹרָה
אַרְבַּע אִמָּהוֹת   שְׁלוֹשָׁה אָבוֹת   שְׁנֵי לוּחוֹת הַבְּרִית
אֶחָד אֱלֹהֵינוּ שֶׁבַּשָּׁמַיִם וּבָאָרֶץ

Who knows thirteen?

I know thirteen.

Thirteen are the attributes of God.

The tribes of Israel are twelve.

The stars of Joseph's dream are eleven.

The words from Sinai are ten.

The months for childbirth are nine.

The days for circumcision are eight.

The days of the week are seven.

The orders of the Mishna are six.

The books of the Torah are five.

The matriarchs are four.

The patriarchs are three.

The tablets are two.

OUR GOD

IS ONE

IN HEAVEN AND EARTH.

שְׁלוֹשָׁה עָשָׂר מִי יוֹדֵעַ

שְׁלוֹשָׁה עָשָׂר אֲנִי יוֹדֵעַ

שְׁלוֹשָׁה עָשָׂר מִדַּיָּא

שְׁנֵים עָשָׂר שִׁבְטַיָּא

אַחַד עָשָׂר כּוֹכְבַיָּא

עֲשָׂרָה דִבְּרַיָּא

תִּשְׁעָה יַרְחֵי לֵדָה

שְׁמוֹנָה יְמֵי מִילָה

שִׁבְעָה יְמֵי שַׁבְּתָא

שִׁשָּׁה סִדְרֵי מִשְׁנָה

חֲמִשָּׁה חֻמְשֵׁי תוֹרָה

אַרְבַּע אִמָּהוֹת

שְׁלוֹשָׁה אָבוֹת

שְׁנֵי לוּחוֹת הַבְּרִית

אֶחָד

אֱלֹהֵינוּ

שֶׁבַּשָּׁמַיִם וּבָאָרֶץ

Prayers of the community priests on the Day of
Remembrance for those lost in Sudan, Jerusalem, 2006

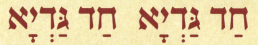

חַד גַּדְיָא חַד גַּדְיָא

דְּזְבַן אַבָּא בִּתְרֵי זוּזֵי

חַד גַּדְיָא   חַד גַּדְיָא

A KID FOR TWO ZUZIM

My father bought a kid;
Two zuzim he paid for it,
Two zuzim for just one kid.

There came a cat / And ate the kid
My father bought / That kid,
Two zuzim he paid for it,
Two zuzim for just one kid.

There came a dog / And bit the cat / That ate the kid
My father bought / That kid,
Two zuzim he paid for it,
Two zuzim for just one kid.

There came a stick / That beat the dog / That bit the cat
That ate the kid
My father bought / That kid,
Two zuzim he paid for it,
Two zuzim for just one kid.

There came a fire / That burnt the stick / That beat the dog
That bit the cat / That ate the kid
My father bought / That kid,
Two zuzim he paid for it,
Two zuzim for just one kid.

There came water / That quenched the fire / That burnt the stick
That beat the dog / That bit the cat / That ate the kid
My father bought / That kid,
Two zuzim he paid for it,
Two zuzim for just one kid.

There came an ox / That drank the water / That quenched the fire
That burnt the stick / That beat the dog
That bit the cat / That ate the kid
My father bought / That kid,
Two zuzim he paid for it,
Two zuzim for just one kid.

וַאֲתָא שׁוּנְרָא   וְאָכְלָה לְגַדְיָא
דְּזַבַן אַבָּא בִּתְרֵי זוּזֵי
חַד גַּדְיָא   חַד גַּדְיָא

וַאֲתָא כַלְבָּא   וְנָשַׁךְ לְשׁוּנְרָא   דְּאָכְלָה לְגַדְיָא
דְּזַבַן אַבָּא בִּתְרֵי זוּזֵי
חַד גַּדְיָא   חַד גַּדְיָא

וַאֲתָא חֻטְרָא   וְהִכָּה לְכַלְבָּא   דְּנָשַׁךְ לְשׁוּנְרָא
דְּאָכְלָה לְגַדְיָא
דְּזַבַן אַבָּא בִּתְרֵי זוּזֵי
חַד גַּדְיָא   חַד גַּדְיָא

וַאֲתָא נוּרָא   וְשָׂרַף לְחֻטְרָא   דְּהִכָּה לְכַלְבָּא
דְּנָשַׁךְ לְשׁוּנְרָא   דְּאָכְלָה לְגַדְיָא
דְּזַבַן אַבָּא בִּתְרֵי זוּזֵי
חַד גַּדְיָא   חַד גַּדְיָא

וַאֲתָא מַיָּא   וְכָבָה לְנוּרָא   דְּשָׂרַף לְחֻטְרָא   דְּהִכָּה לְכַלְבָּא
דְּנָשַׁךְ לְשׁוּנְרָא   דְּאָכְלָה לְגַדְיָא
דְּזַבַן אַבָּא בִּתְרֵי זוּזֵי
חַד גַּדְיָא   חַד גַּדְיָא

וַאֲתָא תוֹרָא   וְשָׁתָה לְמַיָּא   דְּכָבָה לְנוּרָא   דְּשָׂרַף לְחֻטְרָא
דְּהִכָּה לְכַלְבָּא   דְּנָשַׁךְ לְשׁוּנְרָא   דְּאָכְלָה לְגַדְיָא
דְּזַבַן אַבָּא בִּתְרֵי זוּזֵי
חַד גַּדְיָא   חַד גַּדְיָא

There came a slaughterer / Who killed the ox / That drank the water
That quenched the fire / That burnt the stick / That beat the dog
That bit the cat / That ate the kid
My father bought / That kid,
Two zuzim he paid for it,
Two zuzim for just one kid.

There came the Angel of Death / Who slew the slaughterer
Who killed the ox / That drank the water / That quenched the fire
That burnt the stick / That beat the dog / That bit the cat
That ate the kid / My father bought / That kid,
Two zuzim he paid for it,
Two zuzim for just one kid.

There came the Holy One, Blessed is He / Who slew the Angel of Death
Who slew the slaughterer / Who killed the ox / That drank the water
That quenched the fire / That burnt the stick / That beat the dog
That bit the cat / That ate the kid
My father bought / That kid,
Two zuzim he paid for it,

TWO ZUZIM FOR JUST ONE KID.

וַאֲתָא הַשּׁוֹחֵט   וְשָׁחַט לְתוֹרָא   דְּשָׁתָא לְמַיָּא   דְּכָבָה לְנוּרָא
דְּשָׂרַף לְחֻטְרָא   דְּהִכָּה לְכַלְבָּא   דְּנָשַׁךְ לְשׁוּנְרָא
דְּאָכְלָה לְגַדְיָא
דְּזַבֵּן אַבָּא בִּתְרֵי זוּזֵי
חַד גַּדְיָא   חַד גַּדְיָא

וַאֲתָא מַלְאַךְ הַמָּוֶת   וְשָׁחַט לְשׁוֹחֵט   דְּשָׁחַט לְתוֹרָא
דְּשָׁתָא לְמַיָּא   דְּכָבָה לְנוּרָא   דְּשָׂרַף לְחֻטְרָא
דְּהִכָּה לְכַלְבָּא   דְּנָשַׁךְ לְשׁוּנְרָא   דְּאָכְלָה לְגַדְיָא
דְּזַבֵּן אַבָּא בִּתְרֵי זוּזֵי
חַד גַּדְיָא   חַד גַּדְיָא

וַאֲתָא הַקָּדוֹשׁ בָּרוּךְ הוּא   וְשָׁחַט לְמַלְאַךְ הַמָּוֶת
דְּשָׁחַט לְשׁוֹחֵט   דְּשָׁחַט לְתוֹרָא   דְּשָׁתָא לְמַיָּא
דְּכָבָה לְנוּרָא   דְּשָׂרַף לְחֻטְרָא   דְּהִכָּה לְכַלְבָּא
דְּנָשַׁךְ לְשׁוּנְרָא   דְּאָכְלָה לְגַדְיָא
דְּזַבֵּן אַבָּא בִּתְרֵי זוּזֵי

חַד גַּדְיָא   חַד גַּדְיָא

בחוץ לארץ אומרים ספירת העומר בלילה השני של פסח.

בָּרוּךְ אַתָּה יהוה אֱלֹהֵינוּ מֶלֶךְ הָעוֹלָם
אֲשֶׁר קִדְּשָׁנוּ בְּמִצְוֹתָיו, וְצִוָּנוּ עַל סְפִירַת הָעְמֶר.
הַיּוֹם יוֹם אֶחָד בָּעְמֶר.

In the Diaspora, the Omer is counted on the second night of the festival.
Blessed are You, Lᴏʀᴅ our God, King of the Universe,
who has made us holy through His commandments,
and has commanded us about counting the Omer.
Today is the first day of the Omer.

The Journey to Jerusalem / Kes Abba Yitzchak

In the year 1973, on the 19th day of the month of Yekatit in the Ethiopian calendar (22nd Adar 1 5741 – February 2, 1981 – Ed.) we began our journey from the Tigray region of Ethiopia, heading in the direction of Wolkayit.

In the month of March we reached the desolate forest known as the Mezega. Upon reaching the forest we were seized by thieves. The thieves took us off to their hiding place in caves, and began to threaten us there with guns, sticks and daggers, in addition to frightening us in a language that we did not understand. They tortured us and stole from us, taking all our silver and clothing and leaving us with none of our possessions. They also made off with four horses along with everything the animals were carrying.

After this incident, we arrived in a place known as Adi Goshu. Here we were rounded up by soldiers from the Ethiopian army and sent on to the city of Humera. On the 4th day of the month of Megabit (7th Adar II 5741 – March 13, 1981 – Ed.) the Mayor of Humera sent us off to the city of Gondar, located in the Begemder region.

After we spending two months languishing in prison, the Mayor of Gondar sent us back to Humera. Following a brief period in Humera, we managed to escape through the forests and mountains in the direction of Sudan. Upon reaching the Sudanese border, we found that the waters of the Tekezé River were too high for us to cross on foot. We paid the owner of a boat a sum covering each member of our group as well as our possessions, in order to ensure that he would transport us to the far bank. After crossing the Tekezé River, we proceeded to the Bihari Salam River whose waters were likewise too high for us to cross on foot. Once again we paid to ensure a safe crossing and made it to the far side. On the 23rd day of the month of Sane (28th Tammuz 5741 – June 30, 1981 – Ed) we arrived in Gedaref in Sudan on a Friday evening right before the Sabbath began.

Once we had reached Gedaref, the way to Jerusalem opened before us through the blessing, assistance, bounty and decree of the Lord, by the light of His glory and on the strength of the hope we placed in Him. We emerged from the poverty of Ethiopia, leaving behind the dirt and the foods we had eaten, the clothing we had worn, and the livelihoods we had eked out from the sale of equipment for donkeys and horses, and the sale of the donkeys and horses themselves. Having lived with famine and drought, our troubles now came to an end as we emerged from the prison and darkness, stepping from darkness into the light, going from jail directly to the Garden of Eden, from dire straits to wide spaces, from death to life, from the dust of the earth to a fine bed, from coldness to warmth, as it is written in the Torah: He fed them, , led them, guarded them and kept them safe like the apple of his eye without any diseases. He led them in a column of clouds, keeping them safe from their enemies, illuminating the way for

Kes Abba Yitzchak, Atlit, 1985

them by night with a column of fire. He fed the entire nation manna, brought forth water from the rock, and gave them the Land of Canaan. Thus, they inherited the sweet land. Or, in the words of Exodus: "And the Children of Israel did eat the manna for forty years, until they came to an inhabited land…" (Exodus 16:35). "And it shall be when the Lord shall bring thee into the land of the Canaanites… which He swore to thy fathers to give thee, a land flowing with milk and honey…" (Exodus 13:5). Or in Deuteronomy, where it is written, "And in the wilderness, where thou hast seen how that the Lord thy God bore thee, as a man bears his son, in all the way that you went…" (Deuteronomy 1:31).

Just as our forefathers crossed the Red Sea and the Jordan River on foot, we – the tired, blind, lame, twisted and broken, adults and the elderly, babes and mutes, pregnant women – were all taken up by the Lord in His embrace and brought by airplane from Ethiopia to the Holy Land. The Holy Land, land of our forefathers, the heritage handed down to us by Abraham, Isaac and Jacob, by Moses and Aaron, as it is written: "And I will bring you into the land, which I swore to give to Abraham, to Isaac, and to Jacob…" (Exodus 6:8). We stood there on our own two feet and witnessed it with our own eyes.

"Forever, O Lord, Thy word stands fast in the heavens" (Psalms 119:89) – we merited to see these very words come true. It is further written: "The Lord blesses His people with peace" (Psalms 29:11) – and we were accordingly blessed. The Bible also says: "It is He who gives salvation to kings" (Psalms 144:10) – and we saw this, too, come true. The Bible writes: "The Lord shall weaken his enemy" – and this too came to pass. And finally, it is written that: "And five of you shall chase a hundred, and a hundred of you shall put ten thousand to flight…" (Leviticus 26:8) – and this too we merited to witness in reality.

May our mother, Jerusalem, live in peace. May her enemies falter. May the Lord preserve peace in her land, for her nation, her Rabbis, her rulers, and her soldiers. The King of the entire universe shall keep her safe in peace. This is the hope and prayer with which I would like to conclude my words.

(M.W.A)

Members of the community, 1908

The Journey into the Unknown / Beny Fikadu

In the middle of the year 1979, my parents received a letter from the Holy Land: "Come to Sudan, that is where you shall meet him. He will be waiting for you and see to it that you continue your journey from there. We have already arrived and everything is fine. Leave as soon as you can and do not delay."

The preparations for making *aliya* began immediately. Mother prepared food that was appropriate and would be able to withstand the conditions of the journey, and father took care of all the necessary arrangements. They did not tell me anything, but just like mother's Christian and Muslim friends among the neighbors, I sensed that something strange was afoot.

My parents began to work quickly. Everything was arranged very fast, in whispers and secrecy. They spoke in hushed tones to one another and used a sort of sign language that I did not understand. Neighbors who sensed something came to mother and asked her what was going on. They wanted to know why they hadn't opened the store for days and why she was preparing such large amounts of food.

A Small Spark of Hope

These were difficult times in the city of Debaguna, where we lived. The Derg soldiers (the army of the ruler of Ethiopia, Mengistu Haile Mariam) struck tremendous fear deep in the hearts of the population. Every few days they would publicly execute honest citizens who were innocent of all wrongdoing in the town square. Certain residents would falsely accuse other residents before the authorities, just so that they themselves would not be considered traitors and collaborators with the rebels. For this reason we were greatly afraid and did not tell our neighbors of our intentions.

The preparations lasted only a week, and one evening it happened. Mother said her tearful goodbyes to the neighbors who had been like family to her. She told them that we had decided to immigrate to Sudan, in the hope of finding a more secure life there.

Our point of departure was the village Adi Woreva, the village where my parents had been born. There, we were joined by my grandmother, Avrehet, and three additional families. We said farewell to my grandfather and the rest of the family. By the sadness in their faces I could tell that they did not believe we would ever meet again. We went on our way, beginning our journey into the unknown.

It was clear to all of us that the chances were pretty high that we might die of thirst or hunger, be eaten by wild animals or murdered in cold blood by thieves or Mengistu's soldiers. So many dangers faced us as opposed to only a small spark of hope and faith that we would indeed make it to Jerusalem.

To this day my parents and I do not have any logical way to explain the source of the strength which enabled us to survive such an insane journey.

A Miracle in the Desert

After many hours of travel on foot, we rested in a village of Christian monks known as Gedam. As evening fell, we sat beneath a clump of trees and began to prepare ourselves for spending the night there. Suddenly an unexpected visitor appeared out of nowhere – a hyena that tried to devour our exhausted donkey. The adults chased off the frightening hyena and, though the children slept soundly, not a single one of the adults closed their eyes all night long. They were afraid that the hyena might return and make off with one of the little children.

Throughout this journey we experienced no small number of miracles. The first wonder came at the Tekeze River. This river has highs and lows, and when we arrived its waters reached the height of the chest of an adult. After much hesitation and consideration, we crossed the river. Ten minutes

Refugee camp in Sudan, 1983

later the river was flooded by a massive amount of fast-flowing water, carrying large tree trunks along on the current. Is this not like a second splitting of the Red Sea?

The days that followed were extremely difficult: the conditions of the path itself and the weather made it hard on us, and we ran out of food and water. I was five and a half years old at the time, the firstborn son of my parents, Kachasai and Avejo, and an older brother to two younger sisters: Sarah, who was two years old, and Natzenet, who was only six months old. The fact that Natzenet is a beautiful, diligent student these days is itself another miracle.

Amare, my father's younger brother, made *aliya* with us as well. He had moved in with us in Ethiopia after he lost his mother and father and he had been like a big brother to me ever since. Throughout most of the journey I traveled right next to him.

Our thirst for water only got worse. I was the first casualty of the journey. With what little strength I had left I indicated my predicament to my father by pointing at my throat and silently murmuring, "Water, water." My mouth and throat were completely dry. My face became as pale as plaster, and death was nearer than it had ever been before.

My parents hugged me close and saw how I was losing strength. Suddenly, out of nowhere, we found ourselves in a dried-out riverbed where water had just recently run – a sign of life in the heart of the arid desert. My parents quickly dug in the dirt of the moist riverbed until clear, sweet water ran from the earth. The first drops from this river were what separated me from death, which lay in wait for me.

The End of the Journey

We were able to relax completely when we reached the village of Mezega in the region of Wolkayit, where a dear Jew named Desse received us and welcomed us with great largesse. Today, he lives in Be'er Sheva.

Desse played host the way only Abraham our forefather knew how. He slaughtered a goat for us and, when we were leaving, he made sure that we had every last little thing we might possibly need. The Jews of Wolkayit helped all those who made *aliya* from Tigray via Sudan, assisting them with great dedication and generosity.

The way from Wolkayit to Sudan was the hardest leg of the journey. We traversed dangerous paths: through the depths of the jungle, over rocks and boulders – all of which made walking very difficult. My sister, Natzenet, who was carried on my mother's back the entire way, took sick as a result of the heat and the sandstorms, which caused skin burns, infections and contamination almost everywhere on her body. The skin on her belly began to peel, and she was losing blood incessantly. Her screams pierced the heavens, but they did not interest our guide. He cruelly recommended that we bury her alive. "Get rid of her or bury her here and now, she is anyway going to die," he screamed at my desperate parents, who were prepared to suffer everything in her stead.

They prayed for her well-being and tended to her wounds delicately, using a piece of cloth and some water. Perhaps it was the force of her name, Natzenet, which means "redemption" when translated into Hebrew, which saved her and kept her alive until we reached the yellow earth of Sudan. There, in Gedaref, she was provided with medical care that saved her life.

It was there that we also met up with my uncle, Ferede Aklum. The letter that had determined our departure had been from Uncle Negousse Samuel, a young man who made *aliya* before us with Ferede's two brothers (Leul and Addis Aklum). The meeting with Ferede in Gedaref was an experience in its own right. My grandmother Avrehet, who had no longer believed her son to be alive still, discovered that he was making history and helping the Jews of Ethiopia make *aliya* to place where they belong, the land of Israel.

After spending a month in Khartoum, the capital of Sudan, we boarded a plane for Zurich and continued from there to the Holy Land. In this way we became pioneers – we were among the first families who made their way from Ethiopia to Sudan on foot.

(Negat, 13)

The Amra Kuba refugee camp, Sudan, 1983

Death Visited Our Dwellings Daily / Koby Zana

I was born in the year 1979 in Ethiopia in a village named Shi-Wonze. In the year 1988, as I neared the age of ten, I made *aliya* to Israel.

When I was six, the leaders of the village where I was born decided to try to fulfill a dream that was 2,500 years old – the vision of the end of days – and make *aliya* to the land of our forefathers, the Holy Land. The decision was reached in the wake of information that reached the village leaders (which included my grandfather and father) indicating that the paths which led to Israel had been opened up and that it was possible to walk to the border of Sudan and continue on from there to Israel.

The planning and preparations for the journey lasted a few months, during which we sold our sheep and cattle and outfitted ourselves with silver, horses and donkeys. We were greatly concerned that the Christians might notice that we were getting ready to leave, attempt to steal our possessions and make it difficult for us to leave on time, so the preparations were made in secret.

We, the local Jewish population, were outsiders to the Christians. They called us *Falashas* – trespassers who have no land – as well as other more derogatory names. Despite the relative quiet in which we went about organizing our departure, very strong emotions stirred in our hearts along with the feeling that we were about to realize a dream.

On the day before our departure my parents went to visit my grandfather, Kes Medhani Yaheys, of blessed memory, and asked him to give their journey his blessing. My grandfather showed understanding for their fateful decision and gave them his blessing. That night, we left the village and, after walking through the mountains, we came to the village of the guide who would lead us on our way. It very quickly became apparent that this guide intended to abandon us along the way and leave us as prey for thieves and those who hate Jews. We had no choice but to remain in the village. Any attempt to continue along the same path by ourselves would have probably cost us our lives.

We spent four terrible years in the village of this guide. During this period, my sister Tezalu, whose name means "memories," unfortunately passed away. She was born at the height of the preparations for the journey, and since our departure was imminent, my parents knew that memories would be their lot for the coming years and therefore they gave my sister this symbolic name.

She was only five years old when she passed away. She died of a rather common ailment. In those days, though, even simple, everyday illnesses could be deadly, since we did not have any medical knowledge or medications. The pain caused by her passing was almost too much to bear, and it only worsened with the realization that we were being forced to bury her in a strange village, populated by Christians, which we were going to leave behind. During the mourning period, our guide went out to avenge the death of his brother, who had been killed in battle with a rival clan. The witchdoctors of the village advised him not to go, but he decided to go take his revenge all the same and ended up getting killed in the battle. We felt as though the Lord had answered our prayers. This was our opportunity to liberate ourselves. We immediately began to prepare ourselves to continue our journey: Once again, we sold our sheep and cattle, along with our plows and grain, and bought horses, donkeys and food for the journey. We traveled mostly by night, out of fear that thieves might come upon us during the day, or soldiers might stop us from reaching Sudan. My parents hid the silver in the clothing of the children, in the hope that any thieves would not think to look there.

After a month of traveling on foot by night we reached the Sudanese border. We hid in a tent that we had rented, and my brother went out to search for a spot closer to the camps where the Jews who were trying to make *aliya* to Israel were concentrated. In the meantime, we made a fateful mistake. My brother warned us not to leave the tents until he returned to get us. However, when

Camping for the day at Wadi Nakeb el Yahud, on the way to the banks of the Red Sea, Sudan, 1981

the woman from whom we were renting the tents came and told us that my brother had rented a truck that would be coming to get us, we believed her. We got on board the truck and when we arrived at our destination we realized that we were in a Sudanese prison. My parents warned us that we had to behave like Christians who had come seeking asylum in Sudan because of the famine in Ethiopia. The investigators who interviewed my parents believed them and, after collecting fines from us, they permitted us to continue on our way on condition that we bring them a guarantor. This presented a problem, because we did not know anyone who would vouch for us. We prayed for a miracle and were indeed granted one: one of the jailors, whose wife my parents assumed to be a Christian, turned out to be a Jewess who was hiding her identity, and signed as a guarantor for us.

We were liberated but we felt like a flock without a shepherd; we had no idea which path to take. A rumor reached us concerning a Red Cross refugee camp, and we made our way in that direction. There we met my brother, who had rented tents for us in a different location, and when he had gone to get us he had discovered to his shock that we had disappeared. My brother attempted to get in touch with emissaries from Israel, Ethiopian Jews who were employees of the State of Israel and were responsible for our *aliya* to Israel. After about two months, when he had finally made contact, we were transferred to a camp in Gedaref, in Sudan. Everything was done with great secrecy so that the identity of the emissaries would not be revealed. During the night, the emissaries from Israel got us together and instructed us in how we must behave: We must under no circumstances leave the camp, and it was forbidden for us to visit any other camps in the area. It was their responsibility to take care of the provision of food and water. However, because the emissaries were afraid that their identity might be revealed, they came to see us only rarely. When the thirst and hunger in the camp were too much to bear, the men decided to go out and get provisions to meet our basic needs. During this time, some of the men fell ill, and we, the children, were forced to take on their responsibilities. Every morning, along with two other children, I would walk for about a half an hour to draw water from the well, while posing as Christians.

In the refugee camp, Sudan, 1984

After we had been in the camps for about two months, people started to come down with terrible diseases. It turned out that the journey to Sudan was the easy part and the stay in the camp was the difficult stretch which we had to get through. Common ailments, like malaria, began to spread as many people became sick and we had no medications to combat the illnesses. Even my brother became very ill, and there was nothing we could do to help him. All we had left were our prayers to the Lord. While we were still so concerned for my brother's fate, my nephew Avera (whose name means "light") fell ill and died. We were not able to hold a burial ceremony, and we were forbidden to mourn or shed any tears. A few of the men took the body to the cemetery and there they discovered the horrors from previous attempts to make *aliya*: thousands of Jewish graves. We realized that we were in extremely dire straits and that if we would not make *aliya* quickly to Israel we were the next in line to die of any number of terrible diseases. Indeed, death visited our dwellings daily and all we had left on our side were our prayers to God. We asked our contact people to try to hasten our *aliya* to Israel. We

stayed in the camp for about nine months, during which time almost every member of our group fell ill, and we knew that our death was only a matter of time. Our contact people understood this fact just as clearly as we did, and after nine months they informed us that we would be making *aliya* to Israel.

We got ourselves ready within a week. The contact people visited us every day and explained to us where we would be going so that we would not arouse any suspicions or anger among the people surrounding us. On the long-awaited day the contact people arrived and we were prepared for the final "battle" that faced us. Once we received authorization, we went on our way. We walked barefoot through fields of thorns, but our feet, which had already made it through several long journeys, just trampled the thorns underfoot. After about an hour, we reached a wadi, and there our various groups were gathered together. We waited in absolute silence for the trucks that would take us to the landing strip where the airplanes would meet us. Because of the overcrowding on the trucks, along with the suffocating heat and the various illnesses going around, many of the people on board

fainted. We arrived in the desert where the airstrip had been prepared. People began searching for their relatives, and the great pain caused by these searches aroused strong emotions. The contact people tried to calm us – we who had never seen an airplane in our lives – as we prepared ourselves for the flight. We sat there waiting, trying to get our courage up to face the monster that was supposed to land at any moment.

The planes, as they landed, kicked up tremendous clouds of sand and dust that covered us and the entire face of the desert. We fled hysterically in every direction, trying to save our lives in the face of these terrible monsters. After a few minutes, the planes landed and opened before us. Strange people very different from our group, with white skin and wearing strange clothing, emerged from the planes. They began to lead us on board, where we met up once again with the relatives we had lost on our way to the planes. My ailing brother received first aid aboard the airplane. Many pregnant women began to go into labor.

After a flight that lasted only a few hours, we heard the cry over the loudspeakers: "We are now entering Israeli airspace!" Stormy applause and song broke forth and spread throughout the aircraft. We landed. The door of the plane opened and we began to exit. We all got down on the ground and began to kiss it and embrace it, crying from all the emotions that welled up inside us as we greeted our homeland after being separated from her for 2,500 years. Children and adults alike offered up their thanks and blessed the Holy Land. The absorption representatives awaiting us were similarly moved, and we cast one last glance at the terrible monster that had brought us to the country, and we suddenly realized that it wasn't all that frightening after all, and it too had grown tired from the awful journey that we had just completed. Its heart fell silent and rested itself for the next trip.

(Personal anecdotes)

Aboard the plane, during Operation Solomon

Final Surge Before Jerusalem / Fenta Reddai

"Shimeila, shimeila, Eiyerusalem deiheina?" [Stork, sweet stork, how is Jerusalem? – Ed.], the members of the village of Macha sang loudly in the spring.

Indeed, many storks covered the heavens as the spring blossomed. I wondered what was so moving about storks, of all things. I noticed that my great-grandfather, Babba (an honorary title) Ferdu, said: "Did you know that these storks come to us directly from Jerusalem? I'll tell you a secret, one day we are going to make *aliya* to Israel, and then we will realize our dream and you will soon meet your mother, who lives in Israel."

I was very moved by the news because I longed to see my mother again, since she had been gone for a year and a half. I had never even gotten to know my father, for he had served in the Ethiopian army ever since I was born.

Although Babba Ferdu was a wrinkled old man who had difficulty walking, my family and I knew that he was of a sound mind and more clear-headed than any other member of the village. He had instilled a love of Israel in our hearts. He loved to tell stories about Jerusalem and he was able to recite and quote full portions of the Bible. We were accustomed to sit around him in the village as the sun set and listen to what awaited us in the land of Israel.

Suddenly, preparations were quickly under way to leave the village. The houses were taken apart. Food and dry supplies were prepared. Sheep were slaughtered and the chickens, goats and cows were sold to the Christian neighbors. We left the village, along with the fields of wheat and corn, without our Christian neighbors even realizing that we were gone.

Babba Ferdu sat on a horse, with another man walking beside him for support. Along with the other members of my family, I believed he would be able to make it. The journey by foot, which lasted many days, passed through

In the hold of the ship named *Bat Galim* on the way from the coast of Sudan to Sharm el-Sheikh, 1981

plains, over hills and mountains, through valleys and steep ascents. I was afraid that he would not complete the journey. From time to time he would say that this wasn't for him and that he was too old.

We reached Sudan after encountering many difficulties along the way: we met bandits, people lost their way, water and food were scarce, and the like. There were stretches where we had to run, with old people, women and children in tow. We were constantly told to stay quiet.

In Sudan we had difficulty getting accustomed to the dry, arid climate in the country. The people from my village began to miss their green homes; their sheep and cattle, the river and the water that flowed through it, the *injera* (Ethiopian bread), and *sega wot* (meat sauce). Sudan and Ethiopia might be neighboring countries, but they are quite different from one another. We who came from the village of Macha had settled with other refugees in the camp at Gedaref, and despite all our best efforts we were not able to accustom ourselves to the food there.

We refused to trust the Sudanese. We knew that they were scheming against us, just as they had done to other refugees. We were afraid that they might discover that we were Jews. My grandfather Avezao and his father, Babba Ferdu, made sure that we prayed every evening to ask the Lord to bring us safely to Jerusalem.

In the refugee camp Babba fell ill. He refused to accept food and medications from the Sudanese, because he saw these things as being impure, and he limited himself to fruits and vegetables. He even refused to enter the hospital, saying that he preferred to die in the tent with his entire family rather than in a Sudanese hospital.

One evening Babba assembled us all together and told us what was in his heart: "I am happy for you that you will enter the Holy Land.

At the airport in Addis Ababa, Operation Solomon

I am already old and I cannot get up from my bed. Soon I will return my soul to my Maker. When you make it to Israel and things are going well for you, do not forget the commandments of the Lord, including the Sabbath and festivals, and don't stop praying."

One morning, we heard a scream coming from our tent. We understood that tragedy had struck. All of us children went running over in terror. We saw our grandmother crying and we knew that Babba Ferdu had died. We, the remaining members of the family, entered and stood around him, finding it hard to believe that he was no longer and would not enter the Holy Land with us.

My grandfather covered his father with a white *netela* (piece of clothing made of cotton). Grandfather and grandmother, along with the other members of the family, seized their heads and began to lament: "Our righteous leader has died." We cried the entire day. I felt pain for myself and my family, and most of all for Babba himself, who had made it through the entire difficult journey, with all the trials and tribulations, without getting to finally behold the land that he had spoken of night and day.

Two weeks after Babba died, we left the refugee camp in the middle of the night, making our way to Khartoum. We began to recover from the diseases that we had been afflicted with, and it was there that I understood for the first time that the entire journey had been well planned and that Jews from Israel had come to assist us.

Every night, buses were loaded with people and disappeared into the darkness. Everyone wanted to board the bus, and there was much pushing and shoving. Nobody wanted to remain in Sudan. I myself was afraid that the bus would not return the next day, and so I tried to push my way onto the bus with my uncle – but to no avail.

My grandfather reassured me and explained that the bus would be back the following day. When we finally managed to get on board the bus there was great joy. My grandfather told us that we ought to take off our shoes and throw them far away, along with all our jewelry and other possessions because everything that we had brought with us from Sudan was impure and we had to enter the Holy Land in a state of complete purity.

We did as we were told with great excitement and with a strong sense of faith. In the airport in Khartoum was the first time that we had ever seen a plane. We were enchanted and moved to tears. Our hope returned, that hope which we had almost lost when Babba died.

The face of my grandfather – who had been burdened by concerns for all twelve of his children throughout the journey and our stay in Sudan – was lit up with happiness such as I had never seen before. I admired him for having raised all his children in a happy home, and that he had successfully worked the fields in Ethiopia and had proudly passed on the heritage of his father Babba to all his children, along with

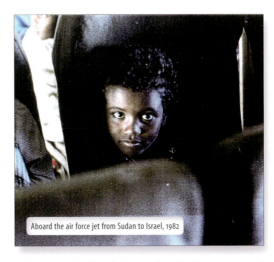

Aboard the air force jet from Sudan to Israel, 1982

a love for the land of Israel and observance of God's commandments.

He was both father and mother to me when my parents were not with me, and he referred to me as *ya'adera-lige,* daughter in my custody, because he had sworn to take care of me as though I were one of his own children.

When we arrived in the absorption center, we met my mother and her brother, who had come along with her. My joy was so very great. Seven years later, I closed the circle when I met for the first time my father, whom I had not seen since the first year of my life.

To this day, because of my great-grandfather, Babba Ferdu, my entire family resides in Jerusalem because this had always been his dream.

(Negat, 20)

Aboard the airplane from Sudan to Israel, 1982

Disembarking from the ship *Bat Galim*
on the shores of Sharm el-Sheikh, 1981

A LIST OF ABBREVIATIONS AND SOURCES

ALIYAH DEPARTMENT: Aliyah Department Archives, The Jewish Agency, Jerusalem.

AND YOU SHALL TELL IT TO YOUR CHILDREN: Ben Dor, Shoshana and Magen, Frida (1999), "And You Shall Tell it to Your Children – A Working, Practical Pamphlet for Passover in the Ethiopian Community," published by the North American Conference on Ethiopian Jewry, Jerusalem. Portions of the prayers are from the Liturgy Project of Ethiopian Jewry, compiled jointly by the Center for Research of Jewish Music of the Hebrew University, Jerusalem, and the Centre National de Recherche Scientifique, Paris.

ARDE'ET: Wurmbrand, Mordechai (1964), *Arde'et – The Student's Book*, Tel Aviv: Publications of the inner circle of the house of Faitlovitch.

BEN BARUCH ARCHIVES: Archives of the family of Kes Berhan Baruch (Uri Ben Baruch).

BEN DOR: The prayer, "Zevezavuk Behelk: That You Redeemed by Your Might," from the pamphlet, "And You Shall Tell it to Your Children" (see above). Recorded and translated into Hebrew by Shoshana Ben Dor.

COLLECTION: Faitlovitch Collection, The Surasky Central Library, Tel Aviv University.

ESHKOLI: Eshkoli, Aaron Ze'ev (1960), *The Book of the Falashas*, Jerusalem: Published by the Rav Kook Institute.

HALÉVY: Halévy, Joseph (1876), *Book of Falashas Prayers*, translated from Cushite to Hebrew by Joseph Halévy, Paris.

HALÉVY, AGAU: Halévy, Joseph (1873), "Essai de langue Agaou, le dialecte des Falachas (Juifs d'Abyssinia)," *Actes de la Societe philogiques*, 3, no.4, Paris, pp. 151–188.

HALÉVY, TRAVEL LETTERS: Halévy, Joseph (1880), *Travel Letters*, Maggid Mishne, 2, 1–2, Lik.

HALÉVY, SARSA DENGEL: Halévy, Joseph (1907), "La Querre de Sarsa – Dengel contre les Falachas," *Revue semitique d'epigraphie et d'histoire ancienne,* année 15, Paris, pp. 263–287 [Hebrew translation].

LESLAU: Leslau, Wolf (1948), "The Falashas," *Edut, Quarterly Folkloric Anthology*, Nisan–Tammuz 5708.

MIZMOR: Israeli, Liora (1999). *Mizmor – Traces From Ethiopia in Words and Song*, Tel Aviv.

M.W.A.: Menachem Waldman Archives.

NEGAT: *Yediot Negat*, May 24, 2004.

PERSONAL ANECDOTES: *The Journeys of Ethiopian Jewry*, Personal Anecdotes, Site of Administrative, Society and Youth Department, Ministry of Education.

STORIES: *STORIES TOLD BY ETHIOPIAN JEWS*, Ministry of Education, The Adult Education Department.

TESTIMONY AND TRADITION: David, Yosef (2007), *Identity and Tradition of the Beta Israel*, Lod: Published privately.

WALDMAN, BEYOND: Waldman, Menachem (1989), *Beyond the Rivers of Cush – Ethiopian Jewry and the Jewish Nation*, Tel Aviv: Ministry of Defense, publishers.

WALDMAN, FROM ETHIOPIA: Waldman, Menachem (1992), *From Ethiopia to Jerusalem*, Jerusalem: Ministry of Education.

WURMBRAND: Wurmbrand, Mordechai, *The Falashas and their Prayers*, Haboker, April 5, 1953.

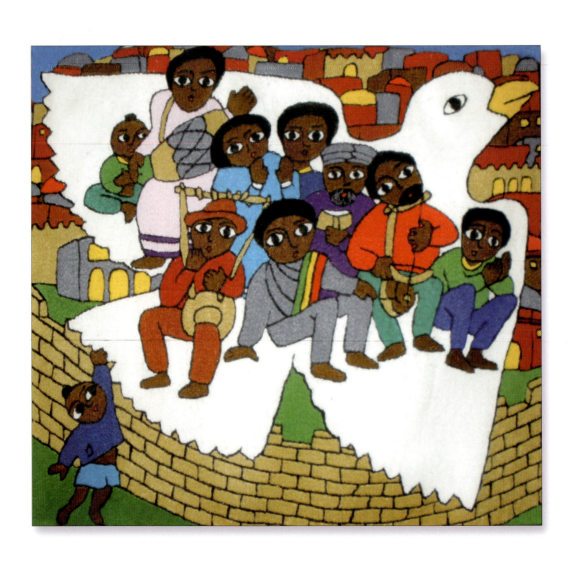

PHOTOGRAPH AND ILLUSTRATION SOURCES

We would like to extend our gratitude to all those who agreed to share their photographs and illustrations for use in the present publication.

We have done our best to locate the owners of the source photographs.

Air Force Archives, 51 (bottom), 221, back cover.

Nathan Alpert, National Photographic Collection, Jerusalem, 54 (top), 119, 120.

Getent Awoka, Ashdod, cover, 17, 135.

Doron Bacher, Ra'anana, Photographic Archives, Diaspora House, Tel Aviv, 18, 19, 34, 35, 58, 110, 114, 122 (bottom), 133 (top), 167, 177, 213.

Moses Bar-Yuda, Tel Aviv, through the generous contribution of the Central Zionist Archives, Jerusalem, 42.

Rabbi Samuel Be'eri, Ramat Gan, 33 (top), 79 (top).

Miriam Bronstein, Haifa, 231.

Ilan Buchris, Giv'at Shmuel, 55, 91, 137 (bottom), 160.

Central Zionist Archives, Jerusalem, 13 (right), 40, 48, 72, 191, 216, 217.

Meir Cohen, Sedeh Yaakov, 52, 80 (bottom), 183 (top).

Judah Dominitz, Jerusalem, 113.

Moses Edri, Mevaseret Zion, 111, 117, 118 (bottom), 183 (bottom).

Faitlovitch Collection, The Surasky Central Library, Tel Aviv University, 53, 56, 59 (bottom), 60 (bottom), 64 (bottom), 65, 72 (top), 73, 75, 101, 184, 214.

Henry Gold, Canada, through the generous contribution of the Diaspora House, Photographic Archives, Tel Aviv, 220.

Dov Goldflam, Jerusalem, 13 (right), 14 (bottom), 20, 43, 78 (bottom), 105, 124 (top), 181.

Andy Goldman, USA, 36 (top), 61, 67, 68, 71, 130 (bottom).

Tzvika Israeli, National Photographic Collection, Jerusalem, 121.

The Joint Archives, Jerusalem, 12, 118 (top).

Gershon Levi, Sha'arei Tikva, 103 (top), 130 (top).

Stuart Lieder, California, USA, through the generous contribution of the Diaspora House, Photographic Archives, Tel Aviv, 38 (top).

Danny Limor, Netanya, 51 (top), 54 (bottom), 189, 219, 222, 224, 225.

Simon Messing, USA, through the generous contribution of the Photographic Archives, Diaspora House, Tel Aviv, 108, 173.

Yared Mulate, Gondar, Ethiopia, 38 (bottom), 134 (bottom).

North American Conference on Ethiopian Jewry, New York, USA, 170, 176, 223.

Office of the Prime Minister, Jerusalem, 102.

The Organization for the Dissemination of Christianity among the Jews, St. Albans, England, through the generous contribution of the Diaspora House, Photographic Archives, Tel Aviv, 106.

Hezi Ovadiah, Tel Aviv, 89 (top).

Israel Puni, Bnei Brak, 188.

Win Robbins, New York, USA, 15 (bottom), 59 (top), 126, 158, 161, 206.

Nimrod Rosenberg, Sedeh Yaakov, 212.

Alexander Rosenfeld, Tel Aviv, 78 (top).

Judah Sivan, Jerusalem, 14 (top), 79 (bottom), 137 (top).

Meir and Adina Sompolinsky, Holon, 76, 95, 172.

Israel Strauss, Bet Shemesh, 124 (bottom).

Carlo Alberto Viterbo, Florence, Italy, 15 (top), 82, 85, 88, 100.

Menachem Waldman, Haifa, 21, 22, 24, 25, 26 (top), 27, 33 (bottom), 39 (top), 39 (bottom), 44, 46, 47, 49, 60 (top), 64 (top), 66, 80 (top), 81, 94, 98, 107, 109, 122 (top), 123, 125, 127, 131, 132, 133 (bottom), 134 (top), 135, 138–139, 147, 151, 152, 165, 166, 175, 185, 187, 207, 210, 228.

Penina Yariv, Haifa, 11.

Dana Yimharen, Rishon Lezion, 26 (bottom).

Ashagre Zeleke, Addis Ababa, Ethiopia, 37.

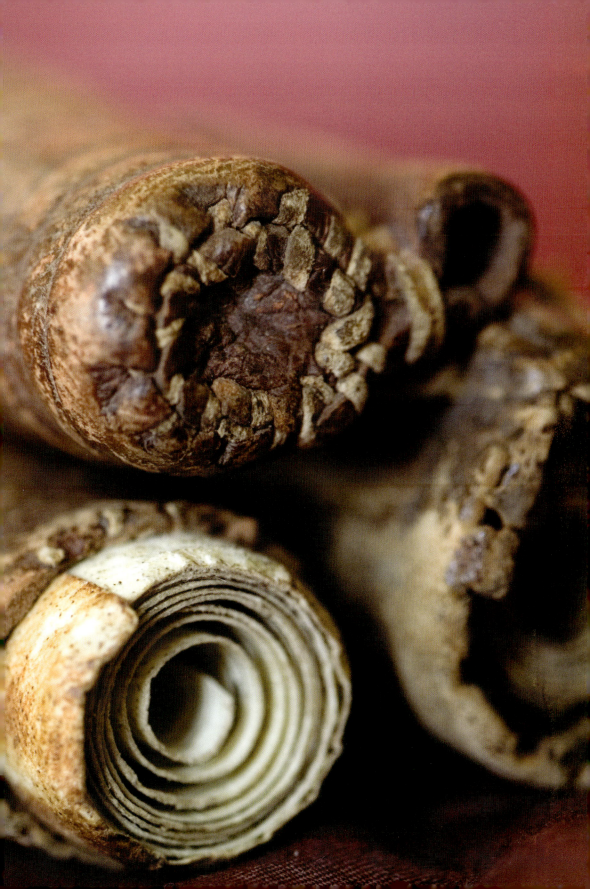